Ribbonwork
The Complete Guide

Techniques for Making Ribbon Flowers and Trimmings

Helen Gibb

©2004 Helen Gibb
Published by

kp **krause publications**
An imprint of F+W Publications, Inc.

700 East State Street • Iola, WI 54990-0001
715-445-2214 • 888-457-2873
www.krause.com

Our toll-free number to place an order or obtain a free catalog is 800-258-0929.

A note about the cover photo: *This ribbonwork brooch is made from new ribbons using vintage techniques. The flat rose was a classic rose used during the 1920s, as were the small blossoms, while the buds—they look like stamens—were used to complete the delicate composition.*

Library of Congress Catalog Number: 2004103290

ISBN: 0-87349-750-3

Edited by Nicole Gould
Designed by Marilyn McGrane

Printed in Peru

Dedication

To my students, who love ribbonwork as much as I do.

Acknowledgments

I would like to simply say: "To all of you who had a hand in this book—my hat's off to you with much thanks and gratitude for a job well done!"

There are, however, several individuals who I would like to further publicly thank.

My first thanks go out to two very talented ladies who contributed to the artistry of the book: Sara Frances for her beautiful photographs and Karen Wallach for her lovely illustrations. After having just shot the perfect picture, Sara was often heard to say "Now, how hard was that!" Think about that quote when you have just finished making a ribbon flower or leaf!

A very special thanks to Kim Sode, Diane Coffman, Liz Morath, Mary Jo Manes, Cindy Anaya, Vicki Jones, Kathy Sigg, Kelly Kiel, Peggy Goetz, Joyce Hoffsetz, Linda Murdoch, Barbara Flowers, Jenni Hlawatsch, Sarah Douglas, and Anita Gibb for all the extra behind-the-scenes support and friendship you have provided me. It just wouldn't have happened without you all!

Heartfelt thanks to:

☞ Carol Duvall, Lindsey Paddor, and the Weller Grossman production crew who have helped me bring ribbonwork to the attention of millions of television viewers.

☞ Meron Reinger, Joyce Hoffsetz, and Janet White for the generous loan of their vintage ribbonwork pieces seen in several of the photos.

☞ Diana Coit of Artemis, Inc and Brooke Exley of Hanah Silk for believing in and supporting my work. The hand-dyed ribbons and velvets seen in many of the photos and projects were a joy to work with.

❦ Edith Minne at Renaissance Ribbons, who continues to bring us the wonderful French ribbons and trims to use in our ribbonwork.

❦ Beth Hill, who continues to paint and supply me with exquisite half dolls.

And heaps of thanks are in order for my editor, Nicole Gould, who not only edited the text, but also calmed me down when I got a bit panicky.

Thanks to my family—Jim and Melinda—for once again bearing the brunt of the creative juices (whether they were flowing or not). Your unconditional love and support are wonderful. I love you both.

Table *of* Contents

Foreword 8

Introduction.. 10

Chapter 1 Ribbonwork from the 1920s: A Retrospective 12

Chapter 2 The Supplies for Ribbonwork................................. 32

Chapter 3 Getting Started: Beginning Tips and Stitches.............. 48

Chapter 4 Techniques: Stamens, Calyxes, and Stems 54

Chapter 5 Techniques: Twisting, Knotting, Shirring, Ruching,
Gathering, Creating Bows, and Pleating 66

Chapter 6 Techniques: Cut Flowers and Tubes 88

Chapter 7 Techniques: U-Gather and All Its Variations 100

Chapter 8 Techniques: Folding Ribbon and Petals 122

Chapter 9 Techniques: Leaves 150

Chapter 10 Bits and Pieces, Odds and Ends............................166

Chapter 11 Easy Projects...180

Chapter 12 More Challenging Projects 206

Bibliography...249

Resources 250

Index 252

About the Author 255

Foreword

Who would have believed that such a variety of flowers could be made from ribbon? Or, that there are so many totally gorgeous ribbons out there to make them with? Or, that there are so many surprising places to use them? I'm guessing that many of you ribbon flower makers who are already involved in this art form raised your hands in answer to all of those questions, but such was not the case with the staff members of *The Carol Duvall Show* … or with many hundreds of our viewers … or with me, myself … before Helen Gibb appeared on the scene. What a change she has made in our awareness and appreciation and enjoyment of ribbon flowers. What began as a one-time appearance on our show has turned into a regular series of appearances every time we go back into the studio to tape. It seems that everybody enjoys watching Helen make those flowers magically appear. Everybody is fascinated with the stories she tells about the origins of their many applications and all of us seem to appreciate the touch of graciousness that Helen brings to every show and every project. How perfect, then, that she would write a book that encompasses all of these qualities and features so that any reader can conjure up the magic on her own, at any time she chooses.

While reading some of the pages of this newest book from Helen, I could not help but smile as I heard her voice in my ear telling me this story, or describing that ribbon, or explaining how to fold this and pull that. If you are one of those artists who some time ago learned the satisfaction that comes from making beautiful flowers and arrangements, I have no doubt you will find this book the perfect addition to your collection of books and papers and all manner of information about ribbon flowers. Here is the one place where everything is brought together in one tidy and attractive package with easy-to-follow, step-by-step drawings, beautiful photos of the finished projects, and easy-to-understand directions.

Those of you who have, only recently, thought about trying something that looks so intimidating will gain new respect for your own talents when you learn what you can accomplish under Helen's patient guidance.

Those of you who are still in the "Someday ... when I get the time ... " category will, no doubt, start browsing through the pages and, before you realize it, may find yourself thinking through your wardrobe for the hat or dress or sweater or jacket or skirt or chemise that would be just right as the background for that beautiful rose. Or perhaps it should enhance a photo frame. Or a box top. Or a barrette. And you will be off on a new adventure in creating before you even realize it!

Enjoy!

Carol Duvall

Carol Duvall
Host of HGTV's *The Carol Duvall Show*

Introduction

Using ribbon to embellish clothing is a time-honored art form. My focus for ribbonwork research is on the work done during the 1920s, when ribbonwork was in its heyday. During this time period, ribbon was used prolifically to make flowers and bows for use on special occasion fashions and items for the home. Not only did the ladies of the day decorate their hats and frocks with these creations, but they made and decorated pillows, lingerie holders, handkerchief cases, half doll pincushions, powder puffs, and much more!

As you look through this workbook, you'll see that you, too, can make some of the pretty ribbon adornments that were once so popular. The beginning of the book shows you vintage ribbonwork samples for inspiration, and then the book takes you on a journey through the supplies you'll need, the techniques used to create the flowers and leaves, and some projects to test your skills. With the clear text and diagrams and the inspirational photos found within the pages of this book, you can embellish items for your home, your wardrobe, and gift giving. I encourage you to perpetuate the art of ribbonwork by sharing your newfound knowledge with others and, in particular, the younger generation. As the new stewards of this exquisite art form, it's our responsibility to keep ribbonwork alive and thriving.

Helen Gibb

Chapter 1

Ribbonwork from the 1920s: A Retrospective

Before we begin, it is important to recognize the difference between ribbonwork and silk ribbon embroidery. While both are surface embellishments made from ribbons, the techniques used for each are very different.

LEFT: A Vanity Box with full set of brushes, comb, powder box, and powder puff, all embellished with ribbonwork and metallic trims. French, circa 1910.

This floral composition is an example of vintage ribbonwork. Each flower and leaf is made separately and then stitched to the background fabric or crinoline.

Ribbonwork

Ribbonwork uses a variety of ribbons in different styles, textures, colors, and widths to make flowers and leaves. Each flower and leaf is made separately and then arranged into a pleasing composition. That composition is then stitched, piece-by-piece, flower-by-flower, to the background fabric. In most cases, the background fabric is crinoline. When the design is complete, the crinoline is cut away, and the composition is stitched to the dress or item for which it was designed. If the item is to be laundered, the ribbonwork is removed and then reapplied later.

During the 1920s, many of the formal gowns of the day were embellished with ribbonwork. One Paris design house, Boué Soeurs, who dressed the European aristocracy, was famous for its lace- and ribbon-trimmed gowns.

This silk ribbon embroidery composition was the center detail from the front of a vintage sachet, circa 1920. Each flower petal and leaf is made with an embroidery stitch. The stems and flower centers have been stitched with silk thread.

Silk Ribbon Embroidery

Silk Ribbon Embroidery, on the other hand, is just that: embroidering with ribbons. With delicate, narrow silk ribbons threaded through a large-eyed chenille needle, each flower and leaf is created with a particular embroidery stitch. Ribbon embroidery is often enhanced with embroidery threads used as stems, tiny flower centers, and leaf details. Occasionally you will find some ribbonwork techniques used on ribbon embroidery pieces.

This well-worn French pincushion, circa 1915, has its top embellished with silk ribbon embroidery stitched in 2mm silk ribbons. The sides of the pincushion are decorated with metallic lattice trim and center-ruched ribbon ruffles.

Memories of a bygone era: pillows, a baby coat hanger, a ribbon purse, a boudoir cap, a powder patter, a hankie sachet, a garter, and a small box all have a small amount of delicate ribbonwork on them. Circa 1920.

Ribbons

Vintage ribbons came in widths ranging from ⅛" wide up to 9" or more. The smaller widths were usually made into charming flowers and leaves, and often used to trim powder patters, sachets, vanity boxes, and more. The wider widths were used to make bows on frocks, and in millinery. Some wide ribbons were often joined together to form a larger piece of "fabric" and then transformed into a drawstring bag or purse, a night cap, or another useful clothing or accessory item.

Much of the ribbon used in vintage ribbonwork was French. The French manufacturers made ribbons (or *ruban*) on looms in a variety of styles and in varying widths. The width measurement was referred to as *lignes*, pronounced line. This old-fashioned width measurement also had a number such as #3, or #5, or #9 (which respectively equates to ⅝", 1", and 1½"). We use these same numbers today to order ribbons. Some manufacturers used, and still prefer, metric measurements—millimeters and centimeters.

A basket of small ribbon flowers on crinoline, circa 1925.

Old store stock metallic braid, net, and laces twist through a variety of vintage items that have been embellished with ribbon trims, metallic laces, and braid. The mesh basket of flowers would have been sewn to a small wall hanging or cushion, or used to adorn the top of a box. Circa 1920.

Metallic Laces and Trims

As an enhancement to some clothing and many decorative household items, especially those used in the boudoir, metallic trims were extremely well-loved and abundantly used. Some of the trims were in the form of antique gold lace and net, while others were solid braids and ornaments, such as rosettes, tassels, and medallions.

The metallics were used on clothing, vanity boxes, dresser trays and plates, powder boxes, pincushions, half dolls, tea cozies, albums, journals, and more, some of which are pictured.

Tiny ribbons make up the flowers in this metallic basket of flowers. Circa 1920.

Motifs on small cards like these were often sold at the haberdashery shops for embellishing use by the homemaker.

Vanity Box with twisted velvet ribbon, silk roses, and embroidered leaves. French, circa 1910.

The Instruction Books from the 1920s

"There is something so charmingly feminine about ribbon; it lends itself to such dainty effects. Small wonder that it has endeared itself not only to fashion but to beautiful home decoration."

from *Ribbon Art* Vol. 1 #1.

Three vintage headbands decorate the open pages of *Ribbon Art* Vol. 1 #1, a popular ribbonwork book from the 1920s.

Much of the instruction for ribbonwork during the 1920s was learned from milliners and from textbooks published by the Woman's Institute of Domestic Arts and Sciences.

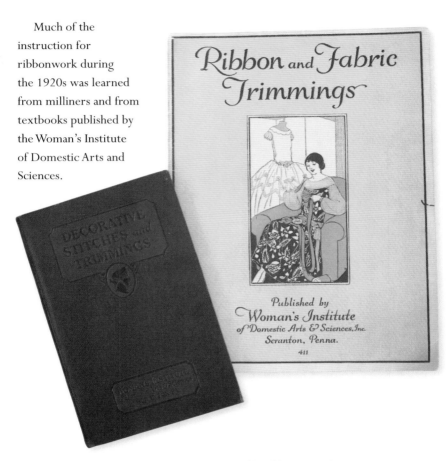

Ribbon and Fabric Trimmings, a paper covered booklet printed in 1925, was a course book for sewing and millinery students, while a black, cloth-covered book titled *Decorative Stitches and Trimmings*, printed in 1925 and 1929, contained many of the same ribbonwork techniques. The pages of these books were filled with descriptive text and one or two pictures showing the finished piece.

The Ribbon Art Publishing Company produced a widely available commercial series of booklets in 1923.

This series of three booklets—Vol. 1, issues #1, #2, and #3—were printed around 1923 and were full of projects made from ribbon. There weren't many detailed instructions, but the studious woman could make the flowers and projects quite easily.

Three antique German half dolls made up as a pincushion, a telephone screen, and a powder puff holder. The center doll and the doll on the right are atop wire frames where the half doll is wired to the top of the frame. The telephone screen half doll has a skirt of gold silk fabric adorned with small ribbon roses and metallic trim. The interesting pillow covers in the background are from France and are embellished with ribbonwork. They were sold as souvenir pillows during the First World War.

A Gallery of 1920s Ribbonwork

It's quite wonderful to actually see some of the ribbonwork that was done during the early part of the 20th century. We can be in awe, or bemused, by what we see, and possibly think, "what were they thinking when they made *this*!" While the Ribbon Art books gave the impression that one should trim every wearable surface and adorn everything in the boudoir with ribbon, it most likely wasn't quite that way. However, according to these sources, one could make any number of dainty and practical things. Some of these ideas included footstools, lingerie sachets, drawstring pouches, lampshades, baskets, baby bonnets, hangers and holdalls, pincushions, vanity boxes, hair receivers, nightcaps, pillows, table runners, telephone screens, and of course, embellishments for hats, frocks, and lingerie.

When perusing the old Ribbon Art books, it becomes quite evident that half dolls figured very prominently in many of the ribbonwork projects. These dolls were available in hundreds of poses and sizes and cost only a few cents. The very best half dolls came from Germany, with some knock-off dolls imported from Japan. The half dolls were made into pincushions, powder puff holders, whisk brushes, tea cozies, milk jug covers, and more. One interesting half-doll project, noticed in the old books, was a telephone screen; the phones of the day were thought to be very ugly and so a way to hide them was devised. Also popular were the bas relief, or flat back, heads about 2" in size. These "heads" were blended with ribbonwork flowers and used to decorate sachets, wall pockets, coat hangers, and evening purses.

We may not want to replicate all of these items today, but there are some projects that warrant a second look at reproducing. How about making a very elegant half doll pincushion, or trimming a hat to go to a special event such as a wedding? Or why not make some small lavender sachets and decorate the fronts with some small blossoms? These lovely gifts would be appreciated by a teacher or friend. A box covered in fabric and topped with ribbon flowers is a must for your bedroom dresser—or give it as a keepsake box for a bride or a grandchild. We can add a little charm into our décor by sprucing up the living room or bedroom with new pillows, all decorated with beautiful ribbons and ribbon flowers. Learn from the past, enjoy it in the present, and pass it on to the next generation.

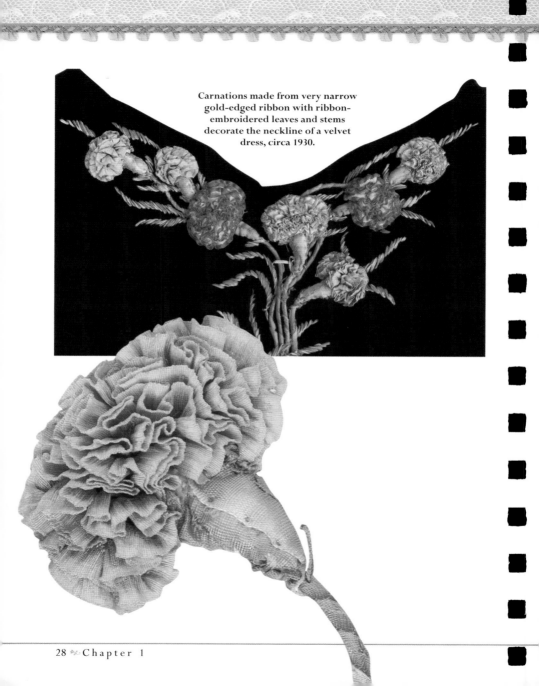

Carnations made from very narrow gold-edged ribbon with ribbon-embroidered leaves and stems decorate the neckline of a velvet dress, circa 1930.

Ribbon roses, double blossoms, and embroidered forget-me-nots on metallic thread "lace" adorn the shoulder (and the back) of a 1925 gown.

A small blossom on a figure 8 "leaf." Note the stamen-like buds.

Cabochon roses made of metallic silver fabric from a gown worn by Hattie Carnegie, 1926.

Silk-satin ribbons were very popular for ribbonwork used on lingerie.

A small composition of a rose and two small blossoms, most likely for use on lingerie, a night cap, or a hankie sachet. The blossoms have twisted petals, and the rose is similar to a coil rose.

Chapter 2

The Supplies for Ribbonwork

A ribbonwork supply box is not complete without notions and a stash of ribbons, trims, lace, beads, feathers, millinery flowers, and buttons. This chapter will discuss the supplies needed and also encourage you to collect a few more goodies such as hand-dyed velvet and silk fabrics, some small porcelain half dolls to dress, and, of course, a little album to cover, some silk prints, and a box or two, and … on and on. Be inspired.

Milliners Needle

A milliners needle is like a sharp but instead is long and very thin with a very small eye so it will slide through the ribbon, leaving no hole. Size #10 makes quick work for gathering and going through thick chunks of ribbon. Other suitable sizes are #9 and #11. Most seed beads will fit over #10 and #11 needles, therefore avoiding the need to switch to a beading needle when adding beads to a ribbon flower center.

Beading Thread

Use twisted beading thread instead of ordinary sewing thread because it's thin, strong, and will gather the ribbon tightly without breaking. Do not use Nymo thread as it is too slick for the ribbon to grasp. Use white thread for the light- to medium-colored ribbons and black for the very dark ribbons.

An alternative to the beading thread is quilting thread in a neutral color like beige, although this thread can be a bit heavy in delicate silk ribbons.

> **Tip:** *Most of the stitches in ribbonwork are hidden in the folds of the ribbon, but sometimes a small thread might accidentally show. If you aren't concerned, leave it. If it bothers you, simply color it with a fine point fabric marker to closely match the ribbon color.*

Beads

A nice selection of seed beads, along with a variety of larger, different shaped beads, is a must for ribbonwork. The beads can be used as flower centers or as dangles in a brooch composition or can be added to a large flower as a dewdrop! Use your imagination and have fun with the beads. They add another dimension and lots of sparkle to your ribbonwork.

Long Pins

The very best pins are the ultra thin flower head pins (they're as thin as the milliners needles) because they are long and can hold a lot of ribbon. Acting as an extra set of "fingers," they are invaluable in holding ribbonwork pieces in place before being stitched to a project. When pinning, use caution as to the placement of the pins—hide them in the folds of the ribbon—as they can sometimes leave a little mark.

Crinoline

This is a very stiff open-weave fabric, similar to buckram but lighter weight. Milliners use both these fabrics as foundations for lightweight hats.

For some aspects of ribbonwork, the crinoline is used as a base to make one flower—such as a daisy, a cabochon rose, a flat rose, a pansy, or a violet. At other times, crinoline is the base onto which individual flowers and leaves are stitched, forming a pleasing composition. After the composition is complete, the remaining crinoline is carefully cut away around each flower and leaf. The composition is then tacked to the garment or surface needing embellishment. Note the photo above of the back of a rose with leaves—additional crinoline has been attached as the design grew!

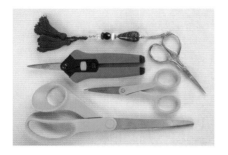

Scissors

You will need two pairs of sharp scissors, or one sharp-pointed combo pair like the grey handled scissors in the photo. One pair (not your best dressmaking scissors as the wire-edge ribbons will eventually dull the blades!) should be used for cutting the ribbons—a 3" to 4" blade is good. The other should be a pair of embroidery scissors with a fine point in order to cut threads in hard-to-reach places, without cutting the ribbon.

Ruler or Tape Measure

A ruler or a tape measure is needed for measuring lengths of ribbon in order to cut it. It is a good idea to have the ruler/tape measure markings in both inches and millimeters/centimeters.

Tailor's Awl

This is a tool used to make a hole in the ribbon or to enlarge an existing hole in a flower center. It has a very sharp-pointed end that gets thicker towards the handle. When a small bunch of stamens needs to be inserted into the center of a rosette and the hole is a bit tight, try using the awl to open the hole a little more.

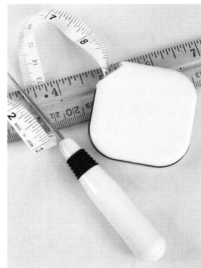

Thread-Covered Wire, Pliers, and Floral Tape

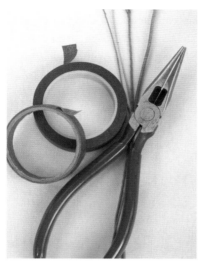

Thread-covered wire, used for flower stems, makes it easy to adhere glue or tape, without it slipping off. Have on hand a selection of wire in sizes 32-, 30-, 22-, 20-, and 18-gauge. The highest number wire is the thinnest wire and is best suited for small flower stems such as violets, blossoms, and rosettes. Big flowers such as roses, tulips, and lilies need a size 20- or 18-gauge wire stem. Use about 12" to 18" of wire for very large flowers, and just 2" to 4" for all the smaller flowers, leaves, or berries.

A small pair of needle nose wire cutters is best for cutting the wire. The pointed end is useful for making small loops in the wire.

Use floral tape to cover the stems if the flowers are used in a vase, or bias-cut silk ribbon if the flowers are used on clothing, hats, purses, or fabric backgrounds.

Cardboard

Sometimes you will cover a piece of cardboard with fabric and then apply some ribbon decorations as called for in a specific project. The best cardboard to buy is matte board—this is the cardboard that picture framers use. It is heavyweight and sturdy and holds up well when glue is applied. It doesn't warp as thinner cardboards do.

Glue

Glue is not recommended for the actual construction of the ribbonwork flowers and leaves. However, sometimes it might be used for applying those flowers and leaves to another surface when sewing them on is not an option. Glue is also used when you're covering the stem of a flower with bias-cut silk ribbon. Brushing on the glue works best. Use the glue sparingly and test it on a scrap of ribbon before applying.

> **Tip:** *If the glue is wet or shiny looking after you've brushed it on, then you've used too much. White glue that dries clear is best.*

Pincushion

If you don't already have a pincushion, you might like to make the "tin can" pincushion, minus the flowers, on page 198. When you have learned to make a few of the ribbon flowers, you can decorate the top or the side of the pincushion.

It's handy to have some flower head pins and threaded needles in the pincushion at all times.

Stamens

These are the little beauties that say a flower is indeed a flower! The best stamens are the old-fashioned, European stamens, which can be found through some mail order vendors or over the Internet. Stamens usually come double-headed in bundles of about 100 pieces. Select what is needed for a flower, bend them in half, secure them with thread, and insert them into the flower. Stamens are never cut in half.

The stamens shown in the photo are the ones most useful for flower centers. Notice that the pale pink "stamens" on the end are not stamens at all. They are buds and are placed beside small ribbon blossoms to enrich the floral composition.

Tip: *You can always change the color of the stamen head with a little dab of acrylic paint in a color to suit the flower you are making.*

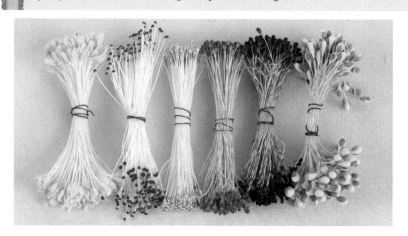

A ribbon flower composition using non-wired ribbons.

Ribbons

Selecting ribbons for ribbonwork involves more than just wire-edge ribbon. While wire-edge ribbon is one of the more common ribbon types that you'll have in your ribbon stash, you mustn't neglect the bias-cut silk ribbons, the double-faced silk-satins, the ruffled-edge ribbons, and the velvet and pleated ribbons. The real beauty in a ribbonwork composition of flowers is the use of a variety of ribbons and techniques.

As a general rule, ribbons that are 1" to 1½" wide are great for the larger flowers, while the smaller flowers and leaves usually need ribbon widths anywhere from ¼" to ¾" wide. The u-gather techniques, folded roses, coiled roses, and leaves will work with any of these ribbon widths.

When buying ribbon, select some main flower colors and some small flower colors in as many widths and styles as available. In your selections, be sure to include pink, dark pink, red, peach, yellow, blue, purple, cream, and green. A yard of the smaller widths will suffice while at least two yards of the wider widths is wise. Buy as many different green ribbons and flower bud trims as possible; you can never have enough green leaves and fillers!

One thing to remember: If you see a ribbon that you absolutely must have but it's really, really expensive, think of a way that you could use just 12" of it!

The quality of the ribbon you buy is important. It's tempting to buy a cheap ribbon to "learn on," but it's not recommended. Start with good quality ribbon, and you'll be far happier with the finished results. Avoid craft-quality ribbon and cut-edge ribbon as they are too stiff. A soft, supple touch to the ribbon is essential for successful ribbonwork.

Wire-Edge Ribbon

Wired ribbon has a very thin copper wire encased in both of the edges of the ribbon. The ribbons can be used with or without the wire according to the particular technique. Sometimes a certain stitching technique requires the removal of the wire if it's next to the stitching or gathering line. To remove the wire from the ribbon, simply expose the copper wire at the raw edge and gently pull the wire out.

The most common styles of wired ribbon are plain, crossweave, ombre, and variegated in widths of ⅝", 1", and 1½". Plain colors are just that—the warp and the weft are woven of the same color thread. Cross-weaves have a warp in one color and the weft in another color, giving the ribbon a two-toned, almost iridescent, effect. Variegated and ombre ribbons offer a lot of versatility to flowers and leaves due to their color changes. Technically speaking, variegated ribbons change color from side-to-side, while ombre ribbons change tone from side-to-side. For simplicity, the ribbons listed in the project supply lists have been designated as ombre.

The mix of ribbons in this basket includes wire-edge ribbons, fancy-edge ribbons, plain-edge silk ribbons, and jacquard ribbons. It's a good idea to have a mix of many ribbon styles in your stash.

A mix of flowers and leaves using predominantly wire-edge ribbon, with filler flowers of bias-cut silk, and ruffled-edge ribbons. The ribbon widths are 1½" for a few of the leaves, and everything else is 1" wide or smaller.

Non-Wired Ribbon

Other styles of ribbon suitable for ribbonwork are those that don't have wire in them, such as embroidery-type silk ribbons in widths ¼" to 1½". Also good are ribbons that have a fancy edge, such as a little picot, a gold thread, or a ruffle, with some even having a double-ruffled edge. Double- or single-faced silk-satin ribbons in widths of ⅜" to 1" make up into wonderful flowers that have a particularly vintage look. Ribbons that are crinkled or pleated will work for several of the flowers and leaves shown in this book.

Bias-cut silk ribbons are wonderful to have in your ribbon box. They come in two finishes (matte and satin), several widths, and a rainbow of hand-dyed colors. The smaller widths are perfect for little filler flowers while the very large (2½" wide) satin ribbons make beautiful roses.

The ribbons in this basket are all non-wired ribbons. Included are jacquards, ruffled-edge, pleated, wide milliner's grosgrain, and wide bias-cut silk. And, of course, there are a few leaf/flower trims thrown into the mix for good measure.

A composition of small ribbon flowers using non-wired ribbons in widths from ¼" to ⅜".

Jacquard ribbons have a woven pattern on one side. While the front of the ribbon has the beautiful floral pattern, the back is a multitude of threads, criss-crossing from side-to-side. Jacquards can be of lightweight taffeta or of a heavier thread and weave. Some have metallic thread running through them. Most of the edges are straight, but some of the narrower jacquards may have a ruffled edge, making them very suitable for edgings on clothing and home décor items.

Jacquard ribbons surround the outside and the handle of this wooden basket while the lid is embellished with wire-edge roses and small filler flowers.

While jacquard ribbons aren't used for making ribbon flowers, they can be used as backgrounds on a project. They would be wonderful going around the sides of a box, as a feature on a fabric-covered album or pillow, or added to a vest. And don't forget to use jacquard ribbons on table runners and lampshades or make them into pincushions, little pouches, and sachets.

A satin silk rose and some yellow flower bud trim accent the red jacquard ribbon that makes up this little lipstick case.

The Fancy Odds and Ends

Small coil roses, folded roses, and curved leaves sit amongst several layered loop bows. The roses and leaves are made from ¼" wide ribbons.

While these photos show a fabulous selection of narrow ribbons and trims, they are by no means a complete array of all the fancy types available. A ribbon stash should include some of these trims as they are the "icing on the cake," so to speak.

Used in any quantity, these ribbons and trims are the little sparkles that will bring your ribbon composition to life. They are also wonderful for edging boxes, albums, and purses, and as extra embellishments on brooches and assorted projects.

A selection of mouthwatering small ribbons and fancy trims fills this basket. The narrow ribbons can be used to make small rosettes and roses, while the flower bud and loop trims are used as fillers and edgings.

Chapter 3

Getting Started:
Beginning Tips and Stitches

As with all works of art, the
preparation of the materials and
understanding of the techniques
play an important role in ribbonwork.
Learn the basic stitches and concepts
for ribbonwork, and then read the
helpful hints and tips for an enjoyable
and successful ribbon journey.

LEFT: A small antique half doll nestled against
a lace cravat displays some new ribbon flowers.
Doll circa 1920, lace circa 1850.
RIGHT: A very precise 1920s arrangement of
vintage flowers using thread-overcast ribbons.

A Few Beginning Tips

⁕ It is handy to have several needles threaded and ready to use in your pincushion. There's nothing more irritating than stopping to cut a new thread and rethreading when you are absorbed in making the flowers.

⁕ Use a single thread for stitching. A length of 20" or so is best as the thread is short enough to work quickly and is less likely to knot.

⁕ Try to work out a knot by pulling tightly on the thread. If it won't "snap" out, cut the thread and start again.

⁕ Leave a good "return" on the thread after it has been threaded through the eye of the needle, enough so it can be caught in the crook of your little finger when sewing and won't pull out of the needle every time you take a stitch. You will waste a bit of thread doing this, but the frustration of losing your thread is greatly diminished.

⁕ Any stitching should be started at least $\frac{1}{8}$" in from a raw edge. If the edge is finished, you can stitch right alongside it.

⁕ If the ribbon has a wired edge and you are going to sew/gather along that edge, REMOVE the wire. The gathering will be much nicer and fuller.

⁕ A note to left-handed stitchers: Please feel free to stitch and fold ribbons from whichever direction is most comfortable for you.

⁕ A final thought: Don't fret if your fingers don't seem to do what they should. Ribbonwork isn't done quickly and it can be fiddly (Australian slang for intricate work). Many times, especially when you're new to ribbonwork, you'll feel "all thumbs." Be patient. Give yourself a chance to get used to the feeling of working with thin needles and weightless ribbons and this "all thumbs" feeling will disappear with experience and time.

The Stitches

There is not a lot to know about the actual stitches used on the ribbons to create the flowers. Basically, if you can make a backstitch, a running stitch, a stab stitch, and know how to tack, you'll be able to accomplish anything called for to make a ribbon flower or leaf.

Backstitch

Many of you might be tempted to use a knot to secure your thread in the ribbon. This isn't the best way to anchor your thread because much of the ribbonwork that you do requires gathering the ribbon tightly. A knot won't hold the gathering—it will pull out. A better solution is to use a backstitch to secure your thread in the ribbon.

Start with your needle at the top of the woven ribbon edge and a generous ⅛" or ¼" from the raw edge. Scoop up a little bit of ribbon onto your needle, pull the thread through, and leave a tiny thread tail—½" is fine.

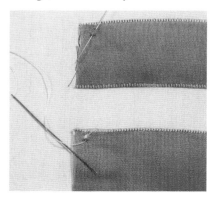

Repeat the stitch in the same spot three more times. Gently tug on the thread to be sure it will hold. Now you can proceed with the running stitch or whatever task is required. When you have finished the required technique and the ribbon is gathered, you will secure your gathering with the same backstitch procedure. Closely trim the excess thread tails.

Running or Gathering Stitch

The most common stitch used in ribbonwork is the very simple running stitch or gathering stitch. It can be used to pleat or gather the ribbon. To start stitching, anchor the thread in the ribbon with backstitches rather than a knot. To end your gathering or stitching, use a backstitch.

Refer to the photo showing stitch length, on page 53. To begin a running stitch, secure your thread into the ribbon with a few backstitches and proceed with fairly even running stitches. Take at least three or four stitches at one time before pulling the thread through the ribbon—the milliners needles are made to do this! You can stitch very close to the bottom edge of the ribbon if it has a woven edge. Stitch ⅛" from the bottom edge of the ribbon if it is a raw edge or a bias-cut edge ribbon.

Stab Stitch

The stab stitch is used when sewing the flowers and leaves to the crinoline or background fabric. Sometimes the instructions might say, "Tack down the flowers and leaves to the crinoline."

The technique is very easy—down at A and up at B. After securing the thread in the back of a flower, take the needle straight down ("stab") through the crinoline or background fabric. Next, take the needle back up through both the background fabric and the flower, being sure that the needle comes out in a hidden "valley" or ribbon fold. Repeat this stitch technique once more so the flower is secure at its center. Without cutting the thread, simply carry it across the crinoline to where the next flower or leaf will be sewn. Don't tack down the edges of the flowers or leaves until all the elements have been tacked on.

The back view of a ribbon flower composition shows the stab/tacking stitches taken to secure the flowers and leaves to the crinoline. The crinoline is cut away after all the flowers and leaves are attached.

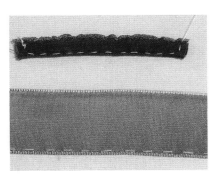

Stitch length varies according to the width of the ribbon. The top ribbon is a ¼" wide ruffled-edge ribbon. The bottom ribbon is 1" wide wire-edge ribbon with the wire removed from the gathering edge. Note: The stitching for both ribbons starts ⅛" in from the raw edge and then goes right along the woven edge. The stitch pattern illustrated is the single u-gather.

Stitch Length

One could spend a lot of time discussing stitch length, but we won't. Simply put—the wider the ribbon, the larger the stitch length, and conversely, the narrower the ribbon, the smaller the stitch length. You may have to make a slight allowance in stitch length to compensate for the type of ribbon used, such as thick velvet ribbon or thin bias-cut silk ribbon.

If the stitches are too big, the ribbon will look pleated rather than gathered. There's a happy medium that you will only discover after some practice.

Remember this: All ribbons have two cut edges—raw edges—that need to be dealt with in the flower and leaf making process. These raw ends have to be absorbed into the ribbon flower technique. Most of the techniques for making flowers and leaves incorporate one or both of the following methods.

Method 1:

Stitch the cut edge so it becomes part of the bottom stitch line after the ribbon is gathered.

Diagram 1

Method 2:

Fold the cut end down into the sewing line, then proceed with the desired technique. Finish the other cut end of the ribbon as per the technique.

Diagram 2

Chapter 4

Techniques:
Stamens, Calyxes, and Stems

This chapter will tell you about using stamens, adding stems, covering the raw edges of petals with a calyx, and wrapping the stems with ribbon or floral tape.

LEFT: A stunning display of stemmed poppies, roses, sweet peas, carnations, and delphiniums—all made from ribbon.

Stamens

Using stamens as flower centers adds realism to the finished flower. Some stamens are used just as a bundle in the center of a ribbon flower and others are stemmed bundles.

While the most commonly used stamen colors are yellow and yellow with red tips, it is often a good idea to mix some of the other colors with these for an even more realistic touch.

A blossom is pretty with yellow, pearl, or gold stamens. A small rosette might use one or two stamens in gold. A larger rosette would use five or six stamens in a suitable color. For a glittery look on a large rosette, try inserting a faceted glass bead at the center of the stamens.

There are no rules for mixing and matching, so create with flair!

Un-Stemmed Stamens

The most common way to sew the stamens into an un-stemmed flower is the following:

Take the required amount of stamens needed for a particular flower and simply wrap some thread around and around the center of the stems and tie the thread in a knot.

Fold the stamens in half and wrap the folded stamens a few times. Secure with a knot. Now the stamens are ready to insert into a flower center.

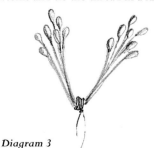

Diagram 3

Diagram 4

Set the height of the stamens to the style of the flower you are making. Some flower types require the stamens to be deeply seated right at the ribbon base, while other flowers look better with the stamen heads showing more of the stamen stem. For most tea roses, the stamens are placed in the "cup" of the ribbon petal, about half way up the height of the petal. On a blossom or small rosette, the stamen heads are usually touching the ribbon center.

Secure the stamens in the flower center by stitching through the gathered part of the ribbon center, catching the stamen stems at the back of the flower. Do not cut the stamen stems. They will be hidden under leaves and other flowers in a composition.

Stemmed Stamens

Sometimes a flower needs to have its stamens stemmed. The size of the wire used for the stem depends on the size of the flower. A blossom would use a 2" to 4" piece of 32-gauge wire, while a large tea rose or poppy would use an 8" to 18" piece of 18-gauge or 20-gauge wire. After the stamen stem is made, the petals are attached by sewing (or gluing) them around the stamen stem. After that, the entire floral stem is wrapped with floral tape or bias-cut silk ribbon.

Select enough stamens for the required flower and wrap the center with thread, as in diagram 3. Hook a thread-covered wire around the center of the stamen bundle, over the thread. Twist the wire a few times so it holds the stamens tightly.

Fold the stamen bundle up, and wrap with more thread near the base of the wire. The addition of a little glue at the junction of the stems and the wire helps with stability. Now the stem is ready to receive petals, or the stem can be inserted into a smaller flower center.

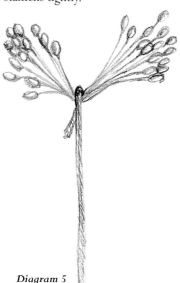

Diagram 5

Diagram 6

Sometimes a flower, such as a poppy, might have a padded green center surrounded by two stamen bundles.

Dab a little glue to the top of a stem wire, cover it with a tiny amount of pillow stuffing. Add a 1½" square of green ribbon to cover it all. Secure the ribbon with wrapped thread.

Diagram 7

Make two bundles of stamens as in diagram 4. Spread them out around the padded top and secure with glue or stitches.

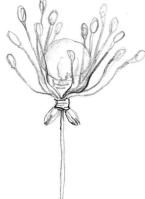

Diagram 8

Calyxes

Some larger flowers will have petals that need the raw edges covered with a calyx. In nature, a calyx is the little cup-like shape that holds the petals together. In ribbonwork, it covers the raw edges of the flower!

The technique best suited for a calyx is the tube technique. Note: Very tiny buds are too small for a tube-style calyx, so these buds are usually wrapped with a 1" piece of ⅜" wide ribbon, and then stitched at the back.

A stemmed poppy with a ribbon tube calyx. The stem is wrapped in floral tape.

Tube Calyxes Ribbon Guide

Use these ribbon widths with the given lengths to create tube calyxes:

⅝" wide ribbon—use 1½" length for small buds

1" wide ribbon—use 1½" length for buds and medium flowers

1½" wide ribbon—use 2" to 3" length for large flowers: poppies, tea roses, etc.

Make a tube by folding the ribbon in half and sewing a seam along the raw edges of a piece of ribbon.

Invert the tube and slide it up the flower stem until it covers all the raw edges of the petals.

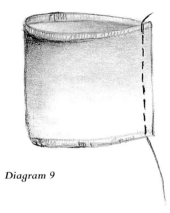

Diagram 9

Diagram 10

Stitch the top of the calyx to the petals and wrap the bottom of the calyx with thread. Cover the bottom of the calyx and the stem with floral tape or bias-cut silk ribbon.

Stems

If a flower doesn't have stamens but still needs a stem, glue or sew an appropriate sized wire into the first few folds of the ribbon at the beginning of the flower technique being used. This also applies to stemming leaves.

Covering Stems

Four options are available for covering stemmed flowers: floral tape, bias-cut silk ribbon, thread, or a silk tube stem cover. The floral tape works well if you are making a lot of large flowers to put in a vase. The bias-cut silk ribbon works best for the smaller, more personal uses, such as brooches, hats, dresses, and pillows. The thread-wrapped stems are tedious to do but are very beautiful! The tube covers make the petals look fatter and are especially good for tulips, daffodils, jonquils, and other thick-stemmed flowers.

Floral Tape

If there is no calyx, place the tape just above the stitch line on the petals and wrap around this area twice, pulling the tape and pressing it so it sticks to itself. Angle the tape and continue pulling and wrapping down the stem. The tape will be overlapped.

Floral tape-wrapped stems on a lily.

Bias-Cut Silk Ribbon

The technique is the same as for floral tape. If a calyx is needed, make one from ribbon first. After it is in position, begin the stem wrapping using $7/16$" wide or $5/8$" wide green bias-cut silk ribbon. The ribbon will be overlapped. Since the ribbon is not self sticking, smear a little tacky glue around the base of the petals and down the stem. The ribbon will then stick to this. A dab of glue at the end of the ribbon will secure it to the base of the stem.

The tea rose calyx is made from a tube of ribbon. The stems are wrapped in bias-cut silk ribbon, as are the leaves.

A brightly-colored pinch petal rose with ribbon calyx and metallic thread-wrapped stems.

Thread

Smear white glue at the edge of the petal's stitch line and down the stem. Begin the thread wrapping at the stitch line of the petals and butt each layer of thread against the other.

Tube Stem Cover

A stem can also be covered with a stem cover. This is a very long tube made from bias-cut silk ribbon. Use ⅝" wide bias-cut silk ribbon for very small flowers, and 1" or 1½" wide bias-cut silk ribbon for larger flowers. Use enough ribbon to cover the length of stem called for in the project.

To begin, fold the ribbon in half along its length. Sew this very long seam on a machine or by hand using small stitches.

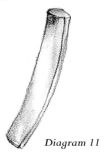

Diagram 11

Tip: *For a neater top end, turn the short side of the ribbon down about ½" before seaming the long sides together.*

Turn the ribbon tube right-side out after the seam is stitched. Think spaghetti straps! Slip the cover over the flower stem and calyx. A dab of glue at the bottom of the petals will hold the stem cover in place.

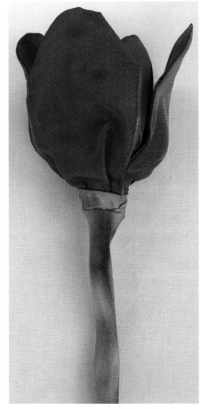

The calyx on this stemmed tulip is of wrapped bias-cut silk ribbon. The stem has been covered with a very long tube of bias-cut silk ribbon, giving the illusion of a fatter stem.

Stem tubes are also handy when a large posy of flowers is made. If the flowers are stemmed, slip a stem cover over each stem as described previously. Wrap the stems under the flower heads with bias cording, or tie with a ribbon.

The folded roses in this posy have a bunch of false stems sewn to the bottom of the rose cluster. The joining of the stems is covered by a very large bias-cut silk ribbon bow. The stems are made of bias-cut silk ribbon using the tube technique.

Chapter 5

Techniques:
Twisting, Knotting, Shirring, Ruching, Gathering, Creating Bows, and Pleating

There are many techniques used in ribbonwork, and it is in this chapter that you'll learn some very basic concepts. These include: **Twisting Ribbon** for stems, flower centers, petals; **Knotting** as flower centers, knot flowers (rose bud), daisy petals, chrysanthemum petals; **Shirring** for edge gathers; **Ruching** for straight / center gathers, ribbon candy roses, and zigzag gathers for a blossom flower; **Edge Gathering** with bias-cut silk ribbon for a bachelor button, carnation, and peony; **Creating Bows** such as single loop, multiple loops, figure 8 loops, shoelace bow, finger bow, milliner's bow; and, last but not least, **Pleating** as for a bouquet.

LEFT: A variety of techniques, including twisted loop petals, loop flowers, u-gathers, and curved leaves make up the flowers in this delicate composition. The ribbons are ⅛" to ⅜" wide.

Twisting Ribbon

Twisting ribbon is a fast way to make stems, flower centers, and even a flower petal. Use a length of ribbon to cover the area needed, in any style of ribbon and in widths of ½" to 1½" wide.

Stems

Start by stitching one end of the ribbon to the crinoline or background fabric, then twist the ribbon in a clockwise motion until the desired length of stem is achieved. Cut the ribbon. Tack the stem in several places, using stitches that are hidden in the folds of the ribbon. The ribbon may also be couched on using matching thread. The flower head will cover the raw end of the stem. If no flower is used, fold the raw edges of the ribbon under on both ends before twisting and stitching it to the background fabric.

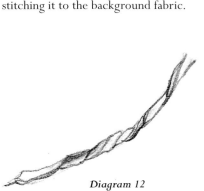

Diagram 12

Flower Centers

Twisted Loop Petal

Tack the end of the ribbon to the center of a circle of crinoline, twist the ribbon, and let it spiral around on itself to form a circle. Take a few stitches around the spiraling ribbon as you go. Tuck the raw end of the twisted ribbon under the coiled ribbon. Secure with a few stitches. Tack the spiral to secure. Apply this twisted flower center over the petals you've already constructed.

Cut a piece of ribbon and twist it at its center three times. A very light touch with the iron at the twist will help keep the twist in position. Stitch the raw edges together to form a petal shape. This petal is used for a wild rose or any fantasy rose. A suitable ribbon width is ¼" to ½" wide in ribbon lengths of 2" to 2¾". Sew each petal to crinoline as you would for a daisy, page 72. Experiment!

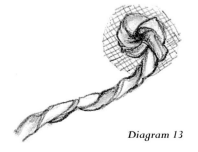

Diagram 13

Diagram 14

Knotting

• Use the knot technique as **flower centers** on blossoms, pansies, violets, hollyhocks.

> **Tip:** *When tying a knot for a flower center, don't precut the ribbon. Simply tie the knot a short way in from the end of the ribbon, leaving enough ribbon for tails to tuck under at the back of the flower. Cut the ribbon after the amount of tail you want is determined.*

• Use the knot technique as a **bud** or **flower.**

Simply tie a plain knot and tuck the raw edges under the knot. Secure with stitches at the back of the knot. It's a bit fiddly, but the result is nice. The three-knot flower buds are made from 1" wide velvet, 1" wide pink double-faced silk-satin ribbon, and 1½" wide wire-edge ribbon. To make a bigger flower, add a few petals and then a ruffle as shown in the plum flowers in the second photo.

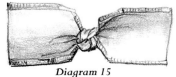

Diagram 15

• Use the knot technique as a **knotted loop petal.**

Two easy flowers that use this technique are a daisy and a chrysanthemum which, when made, are perfect to use on hats. The petal shape will look different according to the different style and width of ribbon used.

To make one petal, tie a knot in the center of the ribbon and overlap the raw ends of the ribbon. Secure the overlap with a few backstitches at the time you are stitching the petal to the crinoline as in a daisy, or when making a string of petals as in a chrysanthemum.

Diagram 16

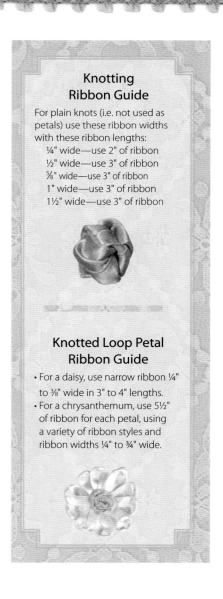

Knotting Ribbon Guide

For plain knots (i.e. not used as petals) use these ribbon widths with these ribbon lengths:
¼" wide—use 2" of ribbon
½" wide—use 3" of ribbon
⅝" wide—use 3" of ribbon
1" wide—use 3" of ribbon
1½" wide—use 3" of ribbon

Knotted Loop Petal Ribbon Guide

• For a daisy, use narrow ribbon ¼" to ⅜" wide in 3" to 4" lengths.
• For a chrysanthemum, use 5½" of ribbon for each petal, using a variety of ribbon styles and ribbon widths ¼" to ¾" wide.

Exercise 1

Make a daisy with ten fat-knotted loop petals and a twisted coiled center. From one yard of ⅜" wide double-faced silk-satin ribbon, cut 3¼" for each petal. Use a 6" piece of 1" wide yellow, wire-edge ribbon for the center. Overlap and sew each petal to a ¾" circle of crinoline as shown. If you are not using the twisted ribbon center, add seed beads or a fancy glass button. For a daisy with ten thin petals, use 4" of ¼" wide ribbon for each petal.

Exercise 2

Make a chrysanthemum using 22" each of nine assorted ribbons, ¼" to ¾" wide. Cut each style of ribbon into 5½" lengths. This will yield a total of forty-five knot petals. Keep each style of cut ribbon in a separate pile in a sequence pleasing to you. Tie a knot in the center of each piece of ribbon.

Take a knotted ribbon and fold it into a loop. Using 36" of doubled thread, secure the thread with several backstitches into the overlapped base of the ribbon loop, so the thread doesn't pull out. Take a second knotted ribbon from another pile and fold it into a loop. Sew the base of that petal with two tiny running stitches, sliding it next to the first petal. Repeat these steps until you have sewn one of each of the nine different ribbons onto the thread. A mental image of the petals hanging on the thread is like that of laundry hanging on a clothesline. Repeat the sequence of ribbons until all the knotted ribbons have been used.

Gather the ribbon petals to about 6" and tightly secure the gathering. Do not cut the thread. Evenly roll the ribbon loops tightly on themselves stitching the base of the ribbons as you go. This coil of loops must be secure or the center will pop up.

Shirring Ribbon or Fabric

Very few ribbons come already pre-shirred. Shirred ribbon (or fabric) is used to decorate the outside of a box, add an edge to a pillow, or if the ribbon is narrower, to make an interesting leaf or rosette-style flower. Any width ribbon, ½" to 3" wide, with a finished woven edge works well for shirring. If the ribbon has wire in the edges, remove the wire before stitching. If you can't find just the right ribbon for your project, use fabric strips. Turn the long sides of the fabric under ¼" and proceed with stitching.

As a rough guide for the amount of ribbon or fabric you will need to use, double the length of the area you are covering. If hand stitching the ribbon, secure your thread at the end of the ribbon and stitch small running stitches right along the length of ribbon, at each edge. This will create a puffed effect when the ribbon is gently gathered.

Tip: *Machine stitching is recommended for large, long areas of shirring.*

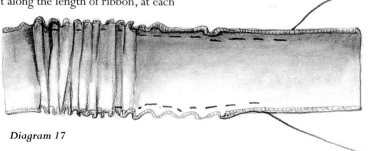

Diagram 17

Ruching Ribbon

Ruching means gathering the ribbon with running stitches sewn straight down the center of the ribbon, or at angles (zigzag) along the length of the ribbon. The most common use for this technique is for edgings on garments, around boxes, on pillows and sachets, or for any items that need a pretty ruffled finish.

In the case of straight ruching, and with a few tweaks, the very simple ribbon candy rose, right, can be made. To make one of these roses see Exercise 1, page 77.

In the case of zigzag ruching, a five-petal blossom, below, can be made. To make this flower, see Exercise 2, page 79.

Straight Ruching

Use any style of ribbon—bias or straight edge—in widths ½" to 3" wide. The ribbon length is about 1½ times the area needing to be covered.

Start with a backstitch to secure your thread in the ribbon and proceed with small (not tiny and not big!), even gathering stitches along the center of the ribbon. Gather the ribbon to the fullness needed for use. Uses for straight ruching include trims for the edges on boxes, pillows, doll dress hems and cuffs, and bonnets.

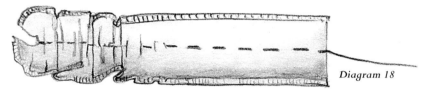

Diagram 18

Tip 1: *If you need a stitching guideline, very gently iron or finger press a crease along the center.*

Tip 2: *If a large area of ruching is needed, for example as in a hem edge, it is handy to divide the ribbon into quarters and pin it at each quarter mark around the item to be trimmed. This helps even out the gathering and alleviates the twisting and turning of the ribbon when you stitch the ruched ribbon to the item.*

Straight ruching was used on the hem of a half doll skirt using ½" wide silk ribbon. After the ruching was stitched to the dress, a pretty trim was added over the center. See page 240 for a view of the dress.

Exercise 1

Make a ribbon candy rose using the straight ruching technique. Straight-cut silk ribbons (embroidery silk ribbons) or bias-cut silk ribbons work best for this rose.

Begin the rose by turning under the raw edges of the ribbon. Think of a pointed envelope flap. This will be the top of the rose, so neatness is a must. Secure your thread with backstitches in the ribbon on this folded end. Sew very large stitches along the ribbon; the stitch length is the same size as the width of the ribbon. Gently pull up the gathering so that large folds are formed. Twist the folds so they are not lined up and then pull the thread very tightly. Now you see the rose! Secure the thread on the underside of the rose. The larger roses look good with curved leaves, while the mini roses look very pretty on top of a figure 8-loop leaf.

Ribbon Candy Rose Ribbon Guide

Use any width ribbon, depending on the size of the flower you wish to make.

¼" wide ribbon—use 3" to 4" length
½" wide ribbon—use 6" to 8" length
1" wide ribbon—use 8" to 12" length
1½" wide ribbon—use 12" to 18" length

Zigzag Ruching

This technique is used for edgings on boxes and sachets, around half doll waists, and even as a flower.

The zigzag stitch pattern is made by changing the direction of the stitch angle as you come to either edge of the ribbon. The easiest way to manage this technique is to think of a "right-angle" or a 90-degree v-shape every time you come to an edge; you will then have evenly spaced ruching.

Zigzag ruching works on any width ribbon and most straight edged styles of ribbon including fabric strips. It works beautifully on bias-cut silk ribbon especially when the ribbon is folded over in half (diagram 20) and sewn to make petals.

The amount of ribbon needed for ruching will depend on the project, but a rough guide would be 1½ times around the area needed for decorating.

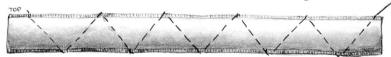

Diagram 19

Whether the ribbon has a woven edge or a folded edge, begin the stitching at the top edge of the ribbon and take small running stitches to the other edge as shown in diagram 19. Take your stitch over the edge, make a right angle, and begin stitching back to the other edge.

Gather to the fullness called for in the project and fit around the item being trimmed. Secure the gathering with backstitches. Cut the excess ribbon.

Diagram 20

Diagram 21

Exercise 2

Make a blossom using the zigzag ruching technique as pictured. Use 9" of ⅝" wide raspberry/brown wire-edge ribbon. Unwired ribbon will also work. Sew the stitch pattern (diagram 19) and then gather the ribbon tightly. Secure the gathering with some backstitches. Trim the excess ribbon under the stitch line (diagram 22). Place a small bundle of five stamens at the center of the gathering. Join the petals together at the stitch line, sewing the first stitch to the last stitch.

Diagram 22

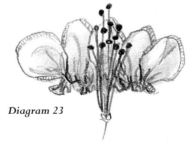

Diagram 23

Tip: *Stamens can also be inserted into the center of the flower after the first and last petals have been joined. Consider beads or a small button as an alternative flower center.*

Edge Gathering

Several flowers can be made from these frayed and snipped techniques: a carnation (right) or tiny dandelion-type filler flower using just the frayed edge; and a bachelor button, cornflower, or small peony using the frayed and snipped method.

This technique is usually done with bias-cut silk ribbon. Using your thumb and forefinger, fray the top edge of the ribbon.

These carnations use 1½" wide bias-cut silk ribbon and the frayed top technique.

Diagram 24

Edge Gathering Ribbon Guide

Use bias-cut silk ribbon in the following widths and lengths to make a flower.

$\frac{7}{16}$" wide ribbon—use 4" length for a small filler flower

$\frac{5}{8}$" wide ribbon—use 7" length for a small filler flower

1" wide ribbon—use 13" for a bachelor button or cornflower

1" wide ribbon—use 18" length for a small carnation

1½" wide ribbon—use 36" to 45" length for a large carnation or a medium peony

For an even more frayed look, snip the ribbon at ⅛" intervals along the length of the ribbon. After the ribbon has been top-edge treated, according to the flower you want to make, simply sew across the bottom edge of the ribbon, about ⅛" up from the edge. Gather the ribbon to one-quarter of its original length and coil the ribbon on itself until all the gathered ribbon is used. Secure the coiled ribbon with stitches, going through all the layers of ribbon at the base of the flower.

Diagram 25

Two small bachelor buttons using 1" wide bias-cut silk ribbon and the frayed and snipped technique.

Creating Loops and Bows

Single Loops

Single loops can be very useful in a small ribbon
flower composition as filler or as part of a millinery
element. Some millinery bows were originally made in
individual parts and then stitched together and covered
with matching fabric or ribbon. Simply fold the ribbon
and stitch some backstitches at the base of the loop.
Three or five loops, stitched in a fan shape, make a nice
background for ribbon flowers, in lieu of leaves.

Diagram 26

Multiple Loops

Multiple loops, with or without streamers, are very pretty additions under small
ribbon flower compositions. Sometimes a "flower" can be formed with a six-loop cluster.
Use ribbon widths of ¼" to 1" wide for small and medium compositions and use wider

ribbons, up to 3" wide, for the larger
compositions or for making millinery
loops. Simply use what you have in your
ribbon stash and don't precut the ribbon.
Decide how long you want the tails
to be, if they are to be even or uneven
streamers, or if they are to be kept short.
Leaving enough tail, simply fold the
ribbon into even or uneven loops the
height you want them to be. Stitch at the
base of the bottom of the looped edges
with backstitches. If you want the loops
to be slightly fanned out, position them
before stitching at the bottom.

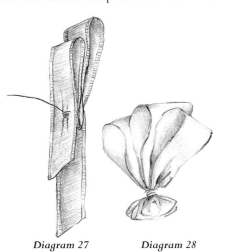

Diagram 27   *Diagram 28*

Figure 8 Loop Bows

These are very useful as fillers in a composition or used instead of leaves. They can be tiny or as large as you like. With only 2" of ⅛" wide silk embroidery ribbon, a tiny bow can be made. Fold the ribbon into a loop and take a small backstitch at the point where the ribbon overlaps. This will become the center of the bow. Make a second loop opposite the first loop and secure that loop at the overlap. A small ribbon flower can be sewn over the overlap, as can a button or some beads.

Diagram 29

Diagram 30

Shoelace Bows

These are the bows learned at a young age for tying shoelaces. Shoelace bows are the main standby for many projects. They can be made with any style of ribbon—wired, unwired, silk-satin, jacquard—and with any width of ribbon.

Leaving plenty of ribbon for a streamer, make a loop in one hand and then tie the ribbon around that loop and through it so the second loop is formed. Adjust the loops as desired and cut the tails in an inverted v-notch or a slanted cut.

Use these bows under, or in, floral compositions, atop hats, on packages, around pillows, or hanging above a picture.

Finger Bows

This small bow was a staple in all the ribbon books from the early 1920s, as these old photographs show. They are rather like shoelace bows, but the method guarantees even loops.

If using narrow ribbon, have someone hold their hands with forefingers extended about 4" apart. Tie the ribbon around the extended fingers and cross the ends near the center. Bring one end around the front of the loops and the other end around the back of the loops. Cross the ends and tie together in a knot. Trim the tails to the length desired and cut the ends on the bias.

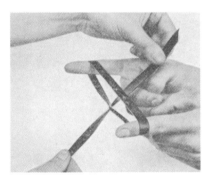

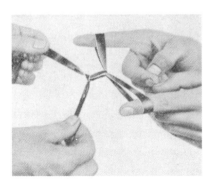

Milliner's Bow

This is a pretty background bow for smaller flower compositions on brooches, or use it on pillows and hats. Measure the area you want the bow to cover. If the area is 3", you will need a piece of ribbon 7" long (6" for the bow loops and an inch for the overlap). In other words, double the area and add 1".

Take a piece of ribbon of any style or width and fold the raw edges to the center, overlapping ½" to ¾". Stitch from edge-to-edge and through all the layers of ribbon

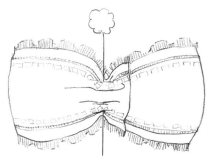

at the center, gathering slightly. Place on the project and cover the center with ribbon flowers. If no flowers cover the stitches, use another piece of ribbon with the raw edges folded to the back to cover the center. Secure with stitches in the back.

Diagram 31

Pleating Ribbon

A pretty edging for almost any project is pleated ribbon. Pleating on very wide ribbon is wonderful for use on hats and in bouquets. Most ribbon widths ½" or wider will work well. The quickest way to pleat is to take a small pinch of ribbon, appropriate to the size of pleat you want, and lay it over on its side. Take another pinch of ribbon the same size and lay it half way over the previous pleat. Secure the pleats with pins as you go. When enough ribbon has been pleated, simply machine stitch or use a gathering stitch to secure the pleats.

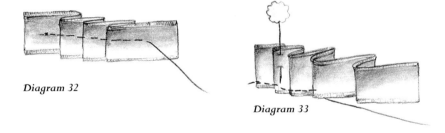

Diagram 32

Diagram 33

Two different looks can be achieved with pleating: center-stitched and edge-stitched. If you stitch down the center of the ribbon, you have an opportunity to cover the stitches with some fancy flower bud trim or a narrow jacquard ribbon. If you stitch at the edge of the ribbon, you can embellish over those stitches with a straight fancy ribbon if desired.

Tip: *If your ribbon is 3" or wider, two rows of stitching work best.*

Pleated wide ribbon makes a very effective bouquet edging.

Chapter 6

Techniques:
Cut Flowers and Tubes

Two very simple techniques for making ribbon flowers are discussed in this chapter. The techniques are cutting ribbon to make a floret for a group of flowers and the tube technique used for making berries and bell flowers.

LEFT: Small tube bell flowers give movement to this charming ribbon flower brooch.

Cut Flowers

Simply cutting out a petal shape from bias-cut silk ribbon and adding some stamens, makes a pretty flower. Two very simple cut flowers are delphinium and hydrangea. Try the exercises on the following pages.

Bias-cut silk ribbon makes a sweet cut flower such as this hydrangea in the small perfume bottle.

Exercise 1: Delphinium

Just one or two of the florets from this technique make a good filler flower in a ribbon composition. Or, make a lot of stems and put them into a large arrangement of ribbon flowers.

STEPS

1. Offset two pieces of ribbon, one on top of the other. Make a tiny slit in the center.

2. Fold over the stamens so all the heads are together; twist the bottom of the stamens and insert them into the slit in the silk ribbon. The stamens should stick up about ½" from the slit in the ribbon.

3. Place a dot of glue at the junction of the stamens and the ribbon and pinch them together at the base. Wrap the exposed stamen stem with floral tape. Make all the other florets in the same manner.

4. Put the delphinium florets together starting with one floret at the top of the stem wire. Wrap with tape and continue adding florets until you have them all secured. Each delphinium stem has 20 florets attached to the wire stem. The florets will take up about 8" of the stem.

YOU WILL NEED

2 yd. blue bias-cut silk ribbon, 1½" wide

18" piece of stem wire, 20-gauge

60 black or white stamens

White glue

Floral tape

Each floret is made up of two 1½" wide bias-cut silk ribbon squares with three stamens at the center.

Exercise 2: Hydrangea

One hydrangea head looks sweet in a small cut glass vase or perfume bottle. One or two unstemmed hydrangea florets make nice fillers in a small composition of flowers.

YOU WILL NEED

18" bias-cut silk ribbon, 1½" wide
4 6" pieces of wire, 22-gauge
12 yellow stamens
White glue
Floral tape

STEPS

1. Cut twelve 1½" squares of bias-cut silk ribbon and fold each square into quarters.

2. Snip off the very tiniest piece of ribbon at the folded center. Cut the outer edges of the ribbon to form a rounded petal shape. Open the ribbon and you will see four petals with a very tiny hole in the center.

3. Fold over and insert one stamen into the tiny hole so the stem hangs down below the ribbon. Place a dot of glue at the junction of the stamen and the ribbon and pinch them together at the base of the stamen head. Wrap the exposed stamen stem with 2" of floral tape.

4. To easily manage the florets, assemble them into four groups with three florets in each group. Wrap three floret stems together in floral tape. Repeat for the remaining groups.

5. Join all four groups together around a 6" piece of 22-gauge wire and secure them with floral tape.

Each hydrangea floret uses one 1½" square of bias-cut silk ribbon and one yellow stamen.

Tubes

This technique is very handy for making berries and rosehips; bell flowers such as bluebells, canterbury bells, and lily of the valley, and stem covers.

The length of the ribbon, the placement of the gathering, and the tightness of the gathering create the different flowers, berries, bells, and tubes. Following are directions for making berries, rosehips, bell flowers, and stem covers.

Berries and Rosehips

Berries and rosehips make wonderful fillers to any ribbon composition. Large versions can be used on a hat and are especially dramatic if they have beaded stamens coming from the base. These fillers are wonderful when clustered and used in a composition of flowers as they give movement to the piece.

To make a berry or a rosehip you will need a length of ribbon, some pillow stuffing or a cotton ball, and a piece of stem wire or gimp.

The berries/rosehips shown use 1½" wide ribbon and 1" wide ribbon. Notice the difference of the ends in the 1½" wide samples: the brown one is stitched close to the edge of the ribbon, the pink one has a small ruffle edge, and the orange berry has stamens and a ruffle. Variety! All the samples have gimp stems.

Fold the ribbon in half. If the ribbon is wired, remove the top wire. If the ribbon is an ombre ribbon, decide which color edge will be the top of the berry (stem end) or the closed end. Reverse the ribbon edge for a different look on another berry or rosehip. If using ribbon that is not the same weave on both sides, be sure to fold the ribbon right sides together.

Stitch the side seam, starting from the bottom and sewing toward the unwired top edge. Secure the seam with backstitches at the top. Do not cut the thread.

Diagram 34

Diagram 35

Insert a stem using wire or gimp. If using wire, make a small circle in the end of the wire and hook it over the top edge of the ribbon. Stitch around the top of the ribbon tube and gather it tightly, being sure to catch the stem (sew through the wire circle, or through the gimp) when securing the gathering.

Diagram 36

Invert the tube. The stem is at the top of the tube and all the raw edges are inside. Before stitching around the base of the ribbon, decide the look you will want for your berry or rosehip; wide ruffled edges or non-flared edges? Are you adding stamens? Look at the photo on the previous page

to see some of the variations. When you've made your decision, stitch around the bottom area of the tube to achieve the look you need for your berry or rosehip, but don't tighten it just yet.

Diagram 37

Insert a cotton ball and tighten the gathering. Secure with hidden stitches.

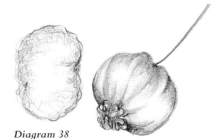

Diagram 38

Bell Flowers

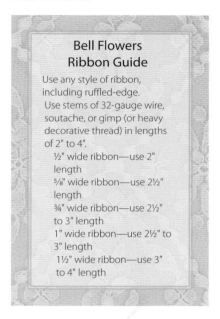

Bell Flowers Ribbon Guide

Use any style of ribbon, including ruffled-edge.
Use stems of 32-gauge wire, soutache, or gimp (or heavy decorative thread) in lengths of 2" to 4".

½" wide ribbon—use 2" length
⅝" wide ribbon—use 2½" length
¾" wide ribbon—use 2½" to 3" length
1" wide ribbon—use 2½" to 3" length
1½" wide ribbon—use 3" to 4" length

Bell flowers make interesting fillers for medium and small compositions as they can arch and give movement to the arrangement.

Follow diagrams 34 through 37 on pages 95 and 96 to make the bell flowers.

Depending on the size of the bells and the different types of ribbon used to make each bell flower, a remarkable variation of bells can be made.

The placement of the gathering stitch at the base of the tube determines the amount of ruffle achieved. If using ruffled-edge ribbon, stitch right at the ruffled edge. If the ribbon is straight (not ruffled), run a gathering stitch about ¼" to ⅜" from the bottom edge of the ribbon and gently tighten so "petals" flare out.

The bell flowers shown are made from 1½" wide pink/raspberry wire-edge ribbon, 1" wide pink/green wire-edge ribbon, two samples of ⅝" wide ruffled-edge ribbon, and two samples of ½" wide ruffled-edge ribbon. The very small bells are rather fiddly to make, so don't attempt those as your first ribbon flowers!

Stem Covers

Stem covers are the perfect
finishing touch for large flowers,
such as tulips, that need thick
stems. They are also nice
additions as false stems in posies.
This topic is discussed in Chapter
4, diagram 11, page 64.

Diagram 39

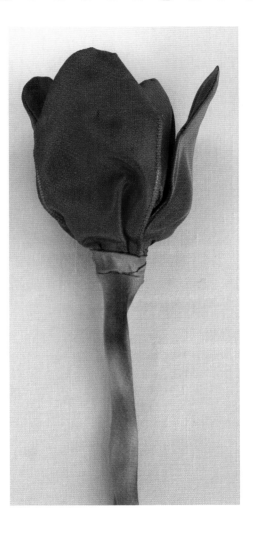

In nature, daffodils, jonquils, and tulips all have fat stems. Therefore, stem covers for these ribbon versions are appropriate.

Chapter 7

Techniques:
U-Gather and All Its Variations

The u-gather is the workhorse of ribbonwork techniques as it is so versatile in its uses. On a short piece of ribbon, the stitch pattern looks like a "U" shape. On a long piece of ribbon, it is an elongated version of the same stitch pattern. In addition to the single u-gather, there are a myriad of variations: two-, three-, four-, and five-petal continuous u-gathers, top fold, bottom fold, and ⅔ fold up, all of which are described in detail in the following pages.

Sometimes the technique will be a component of a flower, such as a single petal, or sometimes it will be a stand-alone flower, such as a small rose or rosette.

Use the u-gather techniques for making fan shapes, petals, rosettes, blossoms, pansies, violets, coil roses, and even some leaves.

LEFT: A variety of techniques are used to make these tea roses. The stamen centers are surrounded by u-gather petals and the outer petals are rolled corner petals.

An assortment of u-gather roses, four-petal blossoms, and tube bells made into a pleasing arrangement.

Single U-Gather Techniques

Petals and Flat Rosettes

If the ribbon is wired, remove the bottom wire.

Stitch the ribbon and gather it to the desired shape. If you are making a petal, gather the ribbon tightly. In some cases the ribbon you gather will be used as a ruffle and placed around an existing rose center. If you are making a flat rosette, continue on to diagrams 41 and 42.

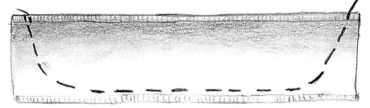

Diagram 40

When making a flat rosette, gather the ribbon to a 1" length and overlap the ends by hooking one end over the other. Make sure all the raw edges are brought into the back of the circle you are creating. The needle and thread will be at the back.

Hold the overlapped ribbon between your thumb and first finger, and tighten the gathering by pulling down on the thread. Secure this gathering at the center with a few backstitches. Cover the center with seed beads.

Diagram 41

Diagram 42

Diagram 43
Tightly gathered basic petal

Diagram 44
Tightly gathered
miniature petal/
leaf

Diagram 45
Small basic
rosette

Diagram 46
Larger silk
ribbon rosette

The u-gather samples shown are all flat rosettes
using a variety of different ribbon styles, ½" to ⅝"
wide. The gold sample (above) is made using two
ribbons sewn at the same time, while the red/black
sample (at left) shows two separately made rosettes
sewn one on top of the other.

The rosettes below use ribbon ranging from ¼" to ⅜" wide. Try your hand at making some of these simple flowers using the ribbon widths and lengths in the box below.

Flat Rosette Ribbon Guide

Use any style of ribbon as follows:

　　¼" wide ribbon—use 2¼" length
　　⅜" wide ribbon—use 3¼" to 4" length
　　⅝" wide ribbon—use 4½" to 6½" length
　　1" wide ribbon—use 7" to 10" length
　　1½" wide ribbon—use 13" to 15" length

For a multi-layered (double or triple spiral) rosette, use 4" to 6" of ¼" wide ribbon. Stitch one end of the gathered ribbon to the center of a small circle of crinoline. Coil the remaining gathered ribbon in a spiral and stitch to the crinoline to secure. Cover the center with seed beads. Cut away the excess crinoline.

Diagram 47
Double spiral rosette

Diagram 48
Triple spiral rosette

Upright Coiled Rosette and Roses

The upright variation of the single u-gather is used for making coiled roses in any size. Sometimes the rose is coiled on itself and other times it is stitched to the crinoline. The pink rose (right) is made with 30" of 1½" wide bias-cut silk ribbon.

The six mini roses below are made with ribbons just ¼" to ⅝" wide in lengths of 4½" to 6". Note the peach rose at the lower right; the center is a folded-edge, bias-cut silk coil rose surrounded by zigzag ruched petals.

Upright Rosette or Rose Ribbon Guide

Use any style of ribbon as follows:

¼" wide ribbon—use 4½" length	⅝" wide ribbon—use 6" to 9" length
⅜" wide ribbon—use 5" to 7" length	1" wide ribbon—use 8" to 12" length
½" wide ribbon—use 5" to 8" length	1½" wide ribbon—use 12" to 36" length

If the ribbon is wired, remove the bottom wire. Fold down the right end of the ribbon and then fold the ribbon across on itself. This is the same way that you start a folded rose.

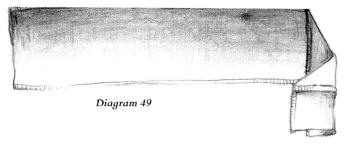

Diagram 49

Roll the folded end into a cylinder. Your ribbon length may or may not look like the diagram. If the ribbon is too short, skip the stitching and just roll the ribbon up into a cylinder to make a bud.

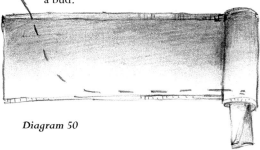

Diagram 50

Sew the stitch pattern and gather the ribbon to about a third of its original length, but don't secure the gathering just yet. Test the degree of gathering needed for the rose shape you want by coiling the ribbon on itself. If the rose shape is too flared out, *loosen* the gathering. If the rose shape is too tight and not flared out enough, *increase* the gathering. This seems odd but it works. Once the rose shape is as you like it, secure the rose through all the layers at the base of the ribbon so the center of the rose doesn't pop out. Your finished rose may be tiny or very large depending on the width and length of ribbon used.

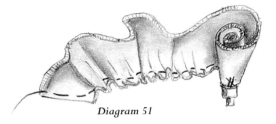

Diagram 51

Tip: *If the rose is large, sometimes it is better to construct it on crinoline.*

This rose is created on crinoline. The coiled center was sewn to the crinoline and then the gathered ribbon was coiled and stitched around the center. The end of the ribbon was hidden under the ruffled ribbon.

Single U-Gather Variations

By simply changing how the ribbon is folded at the beginning of the u-gather technique, you can make many interesting roses and rosettes.

Variation 1. Bottom ⅔ Fold Edge

Use this variation if you want to have the look of two rows of ruffled petals. Wire-edge ribbon and thin silk ribbon work well for this technique. The roses at right are made of bias-cut silk ribbon and straight-weave silk ribbon. Note the top rose. After it was made, the entire rose was immersed in water and the excess water squeezed out on a paper towel. The rose was then scrunched up and left to dry. The open roses were embellished with beads or a pearl button.

Fold the ribbon up by ⅔ or, in some cases, in half.

Gather the ribbon and form it into a flat rosette. Separate and fluff the layers of ribbon. In some cases the rose may be wet, scrunched, and left to dry as described above. This ⅔ fold technique can also be used to make an upright coiled rose.

Diagram 52

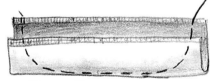

Diagram 53

Tip: *When using any of the u-gather ribbon guides and the folded variations, remember that the ribbon width will be the new folded width. For example, if a ribbon is 1½" wide then the folded ribbon width will become 1" wide.*

Diagram 54

Variation 2. Top Fold Edge

The top fold technique is used to make either a petal or a stand-alone flower. Wire-edge ribbon and thin silk ribbon work well for this technique. One version of the cabochon rose uses this technique for the center and the outer petals. To see the different looks for a cabochon rose, look at the roses below. The first two roses use bias-cut silk ribbon with the top fold technique to make the petals. The third rose uses the rolled-edge technique, page 112, for making the outer petals and the bottom three roses use the plain u-gather technique, page 103.

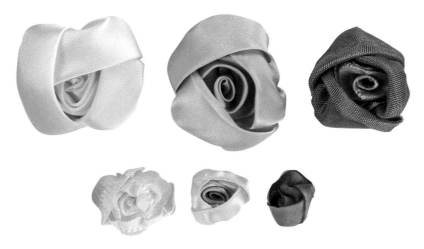

Fold the ribbon in half along its length.

Diagram 55

Stitch the u-gather pattern with the fold at the top. See the variety of shapes below.

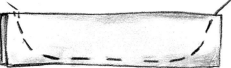

Diagram 56

Diagram 57

A tightly gathered petal. A cabochon rose petal may not be gathered as tightly.

Diagram 58

A top fold coil rose. To make this rose, fold the ribbon as in diagram 55 and use the coil techniques in diagrams 49, 50, and 51 to finish the rose. Make adjustments as needed depending on the ribbons used.

Diagram 59

If making a cabochon rose, sew a coiled center to the middle of a crinoline circle. Arrange and overlap three petals around the rose center.

Variation 3. Rolled Edge

This is a perfect edge treatment for making cabochon roses like the ones from the 1920s. The variation of ribbon choice and rose size makes for a wide range of different looking roses. These roses typically had three outer petals that covered a coil rose center. A folded rose center can also be used.

If the ribbon is wired, remove the bottom wire only. Roll the top edge of the ribbon down very tightly, to ⅔ of its original width. For example, 1½" wide ribbon will be rolled down to a 1" width. Pin at the edges to keep the ribbon from unrolling. Stitch the pattern.

Diagram 60

Gather the ribbon and secure.

Diagram 61

> **Tip:** *Sometimes it is easier to secure the gathering after the petal has been placed over the rose center.*

Diagram 62

Stitch the petal over the rose center. Position the petal base and ends under the crinoline.

Diagram 63

When stitching the remaining petals over a rose center, overlap them so only one row of petals is formed. A second row of petals can be added if called for in a specific flower project.

Cabochon Rose Ribbon Guide

Use double- or single-faced silk-satin ribbon, wire-edge ribbon, bias-cut silk ribbon, or fancy-edged ribbons to make a cabochon rose. The center of the rose can be a simple knot of ribbon, a folded rose, or a coil rose. The larger roses have their centers sewn to a small circle of crinoline. The outer petals use either the simple u-gather technique, rolled edge u-gather, or folded top edge technique.

Small rose:

- ✷ Center—use 3" to 4" of ⅜" wide ribbon.
- ✷ Three outer petals—use 1¾" of ⅝" wide ribbon per petal.
- ✷ Overlap and sew the three petals together so they form a very cupped circle. Deeply seat and secure the rose for the center into the cupped circle of petals.

Medium rose:

- ✷ Center—use 4" to 6" of ½" wide ribbon. Attach to a ¾" circle of crinoline.
- ✷ Three outer petals—use 2" to 2¼" of ¾" wide ribbon per petal.
- ✷ Overlap and sew the three petals together so they form a very cupped circle. Deeply seat and secure the rose for the center into the cupped circle of petals.

Large rose:

- ✷ Center—use 6" of ⅝" wide ribbon. Attach to the middle of a 1" circle of crinoline.
- ✷ Three outer petals—use 2½" of 1½" wide ribbon* per petal using the rolled edge technique.
- ✷ Stitch the first petal over the coil rose center and under the crinoline. Overlap the second petal and stitch it over the rose center. Stitch the third petal over the rose center. The rose is now enclosed.

*or 3" of 1½" wide ribbon

* or 3" of 2½" wide ribbon and the fold edge technique

Continuous U-Gathers

A quick way to make a group of petals using just one piece of ribbon is to use the continuous u-gather. Divide the ribbon into as many segments as there are petals for your flower, and sew one u-gather stitch pattern in each segment. Note how the thread continuously goes over the top of the ribbon edge to connect the u-gather segments. This makes gathering the ribbon easier. Typically you will use two-petal, three-petal, four-petal, five-petal, and occasionally, six- or seven-petal u-gathers to make either a whole flower or a part of a flower.

Two-Petal U-Gather

If the ribbon is wired, remove the bottom wire. Fold the ribbon into two equal sections and stitch as shown.

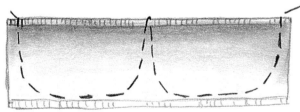

Diagram 64

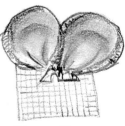

Diagram 65

Gather the ribbon tightly. If making the back petals of a violet or pansy, sew these petals to a small piece of crinoline.

Three-Petal U-Gather

If the ribbon is wired, remove the bottom wire. Leaving ⅛" at each raw edge, fold the ribbon into three even sections and stitch as shown. Use this stitch pattern for a row of petals at the center of a tea rose or when making the front petals of a violet.

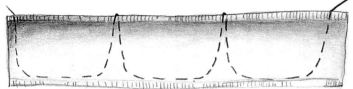

Diagram 66

Use this stitch pattern variation for a pansy. For a realistically sized pansy, use 1" wide ribbon and divide the ribbon segments: 3⅛", 4", 3⅛".

Diagram 67

Gather to the fullness needed. In some cases these "petals" will go around a flower center. Test the gathering to check the fit and then secure the gathering.

If making the front petals of a violet or a pansy, gather the ribbon tightly and stitch to the pansy or violet back petals.

Diagram 68

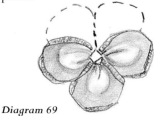

Diagram 69

Exercise 1:

Make a violet and a pansy using the two- and three-petal continuous stitch patterns. For a violet (or "Johnny Jump Up"), use 8" of ⅝" wide bias-cut silk or wire-edge ribbon. Cut a 3¼" length for the back petals and use a 4¾" length for the front three petals.

For the pansy, use 16¾" of 1" wide bias-cut silk or wire-edge ribbon. Cut a 6½" length for the back petals and a 10¼" length for the front petals. If using ombre ribbons, choose which colored edge of the ribbon will be on the outside of the flower. Remove the wire on the opposite side, if the ribbon is wire-edge. Some suggested centers for the violet and pansy are: knots, a large bead, or a cluster of small seed beads.

These violets are made with wire-edge ribbon and bias-cut silk ribbon.

Four-Petal U-Gather

Use this stitch pattern for making blossoms and continuous petals. Blossoms are wonderful filler flowers to add to your compositions. Use ribbons ⅝" wide or narrower.

Blossoms and Continuous Petals Ribbon Guide

Wire-edge, double-faced, silk-satin ribbon, bias-cut silk, and silk embroidery ribbons work well for blossoms.

¼" wide ribbon—use 3½" length
⅜" wide ribbon—use 4½" length
½" wide ribbon—use 5" to 6" length

⅝" wide ribbon—use 5" to 6" length
1" wide ribbon—use 8½" to 12" length
1½" wide ribbon—use 16" to 20" length

These blossoms reflect different styles and sizes of ribbon. Above: ½" wide embroidery silk ribbon, ⅜" wide double-faced silk-satin. Facing page: ⅛" wide vintage fine grosgrain, ¼" wide vintage metallic ribbon, ¼" wide silk embroidery ribbon.

If the ribbon is wired, remove the bottom wire. Fold the ribbon into four equal sections and stitch as shown.

Diagram 70

Diagram 71

If making blossoms, regardless of the ribbon style or size used, gather tightly to form four petals. Join the first and last petals together. Note: If using stamens for the center, insert the stamens before joining the petals together. The stamen stems can be left long as they will be hidden under other flowers and leaves in a composition. Or, they can be coiled on themselves and secured with stitches at the back of the blossom. If using beads for the center, add the beads after the petals are joined. The blossom will look different according to the ribbon used.

If the petals are to be used on a tea rose, do not secure the gathering until the petals have been fitted around the rose center.

Five-Petal U-Gather

Use this stitch pattern for making five-petal blossoms. Use the same ribbon width guide as for four-petal blossoms, but increase the ribbon length by one segment.

If the ribbon is wired, remove the bottom wire. Fold the ribbon into five sections and stitch as shown. Gather the ribbon.

Diagram 72

Adjust the gathering around the flower center and secure the gathering. Join the petals.

Note: In some cases the petals are stitched and joined together first and a separate rose center is placed on top of the petals.

Diagram 73

Variations for Continuous U-gathers

As with single u-gathers, the continuous u-gathers can have variations too. These are:

Variation 1. Bottom ⅔ Fold Edge

Use for any continuous stitch pattern. Shown is the four-petal version. Fold the ribbon up ⅔ and stitch the pattern desired. Gather to the fullness needed to fit around the flower center. Join the petals together after placing them around the flower center.

Diagram 74

Variation 2. Top Fold Edge

Use for any continuous stitch pattern. Fold the ribbon in half along its length with the fold edge at the top. Fold the raw edge of the ribbon down on the right end and then make a coil. Secure the coil with stitches. Without cutting the thread, divide the remaining ribbon into equal segments and sew the continuous stitch pattern as called for in a particular project. A very attractive rose can be made with this technique with at least seven continuous segments.

Continue on with other segments

Diagram 75

Chapter 8

Techniques:

Folding Ribbon and Petals

This chapter focuses on the variety of ways that ribbon can be folded, either to make a complete flower or to make one component of a flower, such as a petal.

Included in the complete flower techniques are: basic bud, fuchsia, vintage flat rose, and folded rose. Included in the folding ribbon as a component of a flower are: dipped corner petals, rolled corner petals, pinch petals, and gothic arch.

LEFT: Tea roses are best made with the rolled corner petal technique. Mixing the ribbon colors within each rose gives life to the flower.

Folding Ribbon

The basic bud, fuchsia, vintage flat rose, and folded rose are perfect examples of folding ribbon into a complete flower.

Basic Bud

Use these small buds as fillers in a composition. They are also attractive as dangling buds, à la the 1920s. When using ombre ribbon, you have a choice of edge color as shown in the photo on this page. For another example of this bud, see the brooch project on page 209.

Basic Bud Ribbon Guide

Use any style of ribbon:
   ⅝" wide ribbon—use 2" length
   1" wide ribbon use—use 2½" length
   1½" wide ribbon—use 4" length
   2½" wide ribbon—use 5" to 6" length

Fold the ribbon across itself as shown. It's a bit like giving yourself a hug! Also note that this same diagram can be used to make a leaf using any style of ribbon. Simply fold the ribbon and gather across the bottom.

Diagram 76

Curl the left edge of the ribbon. Pin to hold in place. If stemming the bud, insert a 3" piece of wire or gimp between the layers of ribbon so it's caught in the stitching that follows.

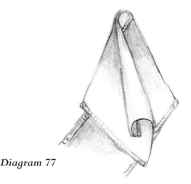

Diagram 77

Stitch and gather across the layers of ribbon as shown. Pull the gathering tightly, wrap the thread once around the stitching, and secure.

Diagram 78

If the bud is exposed in a composition, it will need a calyx. Refer to Chapter 4, diagrams 9 and 10, page 61 for buds needing a larger calyx. If the bud is very small, use a 1" piece of ⅜" wide ribbon and wrap this around the raw edges and secure it in the back of the bud with a few stitches.

Diagram 79

Fuchsia

Fuchsias may be used alone in a composition of flowers or in a cluster. The hanging thread stem is usually left plain if the flower is to be stitched tightly into a composition. If the fuchsias will dangle, decorative thread or beaded stems are very attractive.

Fuchsia Ribbon Guide

Use any style of ribbon and three double-headed stamens:
   ¾" wide ribbon—use 2¾" length
   1" wide ribbon—use 3" length
   1½" wide ribbon—use 5¼" length

The two top fuchsias were made using 1" wide wire-edge ribbon and the two flowers below with non-wired ribbon.

Overlap the ribbon ¼" so it forms a tube shape. Secure the thread into the ribbon at the center. Lay three stamens across the center of the overlapped ribbon and sew the stamens through the overlapped layers. Cut the thread.

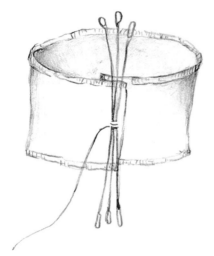

Diagram 80

Flatten the ribbon so the stamens are in the center. Secure the thread into the long edge of the ribbon (avoiding the stamens!) and stitch the diamond stitch pattern, being sure to go over the edges of the ribbon as shown. Pull the gathering very tightly, and the ribbon will form a dome shape with "wings"; these are the petals. Secure the gathering with backstitches and run the threaded needle up into the dome shape and out the top of the flower. Leave a 9" thread allowance and cut. Depending on how you use the fuchsia, this thread may be beaded or left plain for sewing the flower to the project. Style the flower by fluffing out the petals.

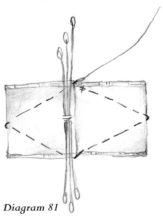

Diagram 81

Vintage Flat Rose

Widely used on many items during the 1920s (and much beloved by the ladies of the day) these roses were made in many sizes using straight-edge styles of ribbon. The rose is made from one length of ribbon that is turned to create folds and then stitched to a circle of crinoline. It isn't hard to make, but it takes a moment or two to grasp the idea.

Vintage Flat Rose Ribbon Guide

Use any style of ribbon that has a straight edge. The finished rose sizes are approximate.

⅜" wide ribbon—use 5" to 7" length for a maximum rose diameter of ¾".

⅝" wide ribbon—use 6" to 12" length for a maximum rose diameter of 1¼".

1" wide ribbon—use 12" to 18" length for a maximum rose diameter of 2".

1½" wide ribbon—use 22" to 27" length for a maximum rose diameter of 3".

These vintage-style flat roses show wire-edge ribbon and double-faced satin-silk ribbon in widths of ⅝" wide and 1" wide. How much ribbon you use is somewhat governed by its width, as indicated in the ribbon guide.

Tip: *It's easier not to cut the ribbon beforehand but to simply make the rose to the size you need, and then cut the ribbon.*

Cut a circle of crinoline. The circle size is approximately twice the width
of the ribbon being used; it can always be cut down if the rose is smaller than
planned. Make a knot at the end of a length of ribbon. Sew the knot to the center
of the crinoline circle. Sew a stitch beside the top right corner of the knot. This
will act as a pivot when turning the ribbon tail to make the first fold. With your
finger and thumb, hold the ribbon at this stitch and turn the ribbon down to near
the short knot tail so a fold is created.

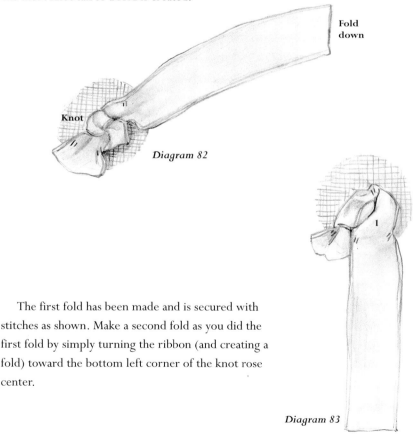

**Fold
down**

Knot

Diagram 82

The first fold has been made and is secured with
stitches as shown. Make a second fold as you did the
first fold by simply turning the ribbon (and creating a
fold) toward the bottom left corner of the knot rose
center.

Diagram 83

The second fold has been made and is secured with stitches as shown. Turn the ribbon and create another fold.

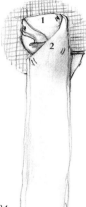

Diagram 84

The third fold has been made and is secured with stitches as shown. Turn the ribbon and create a fourth fold.

Diagram 85

The fourth fold has been made and is secured with stitches as shown. You have completed one round of folds. Continue to turn the ribbon and make folds until all the ribbon is used or until the desired size for your rose is reached. To finish the rose, cut the ribbon and tuck the raw edges to the underside of the crinoline. In most cases, the outer row of folds will hang over the edge of the crinoline circle. Tack this excess ribbon under the circle.

Diagram 86

Folded Rose

Folded roses are the classic rose of this modern age and, while not hard to make, are a bit like the vintage flat rose and just a bit tricky to grasp at first. However, once you've mastered the technique, you will be folding every ribbon in sight!

Use any width and length of ribbon to make this rose, although you will soon find that the size of the rose is somewhat limited by the ribbon width. A very large folded rose can be made with one yard of 1½" wide ribbon, while a smaller rose may only take 18" of ribbon. The smaller the ribbon width and length, the smaller the rose will be. Experiment or review some of the projects for rose sizes.

This large folded rose is made of 1½" wide wire-edge ribbon.

The folded roses shown are made from several styles and widths of ribbon:. The large lavender rose uses 1" wire-edge ribbon; the dark pink rose uses a short length of 1" wire-edge ribbon; the mauve rose uses ⅝" wide double-ruffled ribbon; the pale pink rose uses ⅝" wide single-faced silk-satin ribbon; and the yellow rose uses ⅛" wide double-faced silk-satin ribbon.

Fold down the right end of the ribbon.

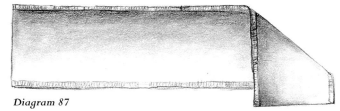

Diagram 87

Fold the ribbon across once.

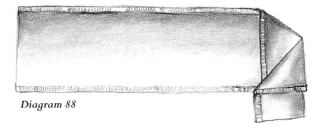

Diagram 88

Tightly roll the ribbon until the top of it forms a round cylinder. These rolls are the secret to beautiful rose centers. Stitch the base to secure ribbon folds. Do not cut the thread.

Fold the ribbon on the left, toward the back. Tilt the coiled ribbon cylinder so it rests almost at the end of the diagonal fold. A large gap should be evident between the fold and the cylinder—this is good! The top of the cylinder should not rise higher than the folded edge of the ribbon.

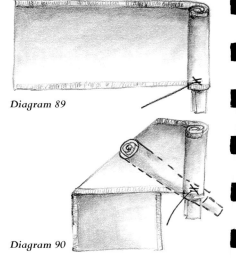

Diagram 89

Diagram 90

Roll the ribbon cylinder beyond the diagonal until the excess ribbon is situated to the left of the cylinder again. Secure the new folds of the ribbon cylinder. You'll notice that these folds at the base of the rose will creep up higher and higher as the rose grows. Remember to keep the top folds of this rose level in order to avoid the dreaded telescoping rose center! Repeat diagrams 90 through 91 until the desired size of rose is reached.

Finish the rose by folding down the last few inches of ribbon into the base of the rose and securing with stitches. Trim the excess ribbon from the base of the rose. If the ribbon is wired, style the rose by pinching the top edges of the ribbon.

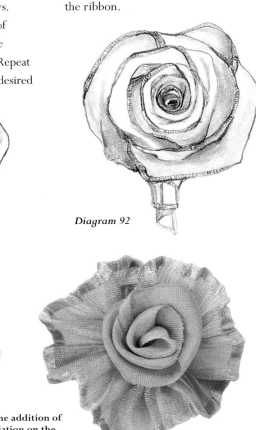

Diagram 91

Diagram 92

These small folded roses have the addition of a gathered ruffle. For more variation on the folded rose technique, see the following pages.

Variation 1. Folded Rose with Gathered Extension

This variation is nice to use for small flowers as it gives the rose a completely different character. As shown in the photo, the pink rose was made using ⅝" wide ruffled-edge ribbon.

Make the folded rose following diagrams 87 through 91. Depending on the size of the ribbon used and the amount of gathering needed, gather the remaining length of ribbon and coil the gathering around the folded rose. Secure the coiling with stitches and trim the thread and any excess ribbon from the base of the rose.

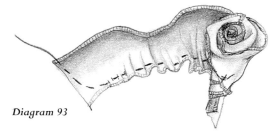

Diagram 93

Variation 2. Thread Sculpted Folded Rose

Make the folded rose following diagrams 87 through 92. Closely trim the base of the rose and stitch it to the crinoline in the composition you are making. Begin the "sculpting" by bringing your thread and needle from under the crinoline to the section of the rose ribbon fold that you want to shape.

Catch the ribbon with the needle and bring the needle back down to the underside of the crinoline. Repeat this for all areas of the rose that you want to sculpt or shape. If you make a mistake, simply unpick the offending threads and re-stitch. This sculpting technique may be done to any style of rose: coil rose, petal rose, etc.

Diagram 94

Diagram 95

Sculpting Tip: *Don't strive for perfection, as no two roses will look the same.*

Petals

Making petals is as simple as folding a piece of ribbon and rounding off the top corners with a little roll here, a tuck there, and a little gathering at the bottom, so a petal shape emerges. These special ribbon petals make the flowers look very realistic. The following petals are described in this chapter: dipped corner, rolled corner, pinched, and gothic arch.

Dipped Corner

This is a very easy corner treatment for simple roses and gardenias.

Fold the ribbon in half. Tack both sides of the ribbon, approximately ¼" down (½" if using 1½" wide ribbon) from the fold.

Turn the ribbon right-side out, keeping the corners tucked in.

Diagram 96

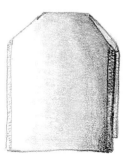

Diagram 97

Narrow the bottom of the ribbon with a single pleat and stitch in place.

Diagram 98

As this illustration shows, if the petals are not to be sewn to stamens or stemmed, sew them to a ½" circle of crinoline, overlapping them so they fit into one row. Cover the center with rosettes, buttons, or larger beads.

If the flower you are making uses stamens, like the wild rose in the photo on the facing page, sew the first petal to the stamens and then sew on the remaining petals so one row of petals is formed.

Diagram 99

Dipped Corner Petals Ribbon Guide

1" wide ribbon—use 2" to 3" length
1½" wide ribbon—use 2½" to 4½" length

Rolled Corner

This is the very best petal technique to use for tea roses as they give the flower such a realistic look.

Fold the ribbon in half.

Diagram 100

Work on the back of the petal first. Fold the ribbon in one corner. The size of this fold will determine if the finished petal is round-topped or pointed. Small corners will give a more rounded petal shape.

Diagram 101

Roll this corner again. Secure the roll with a few hidden backstitches from beneath the roll of ribbon. Sometimes it is easier to open the layers of ribbon and make these stitches from the inside. Be careful not to let the stitches show on the front of the petal. Secure the stitches and cut the thread.

Diagram 102

Fold in the other corner.

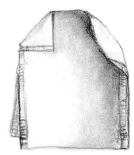

Diagram 103

Narrow the bottom of the petal with two pleats. Secure with stitches. This is the back view of the completed petal.

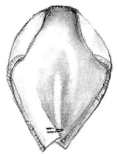

Diagram 105

Roll this corner again. Secure the roll with a few hidden backstitches from beneath the roll of ribbon. Cut the thread.

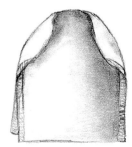

Diagram 104

Front view of completed petal. The petal will be cupped.

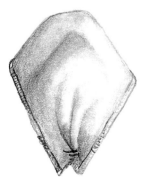

Diagram 106

If making a rose that is not stemmed, stitch the first petal to the rose center, keeping the tops of the petals above the top of the rose center. Evenly arrange the remaining petals to fit in the first row.

If making a large tea rose, as in the photo on page 138, stitch the first petal to the rose center/stamens and then stitch each consecutive petal to the previous petal, continuing in a clockwise manner until all the petals have been stitched on. The tops of the petals should be positioned slightly higher than the top of the rose center. To secure and tighten the rose, push the needle and thread through all the layers of ribbon near the base of the rose several times. Secure the stitches and trim the excess ribbon from the base.

Diagram 107

Rolled Corner Petals Ribbon Guide

Suitable ribbon styles are bias-cut silk ribbon, wire-edge ribbon, and thin embroidery silk ribbon. Use the smaller length of ribbon for the inner rows of petals and the large lengths for the outer rows of petals.

    1" wide ribbon—use 2" to 3" length for each petal
    1½" wide ribbon—use 2½" to 4½" length for each petal

The blended tea rose uses u-gather petals at the center and rolled corner petals for the outer petals.

Exercise: Blended Tea Rose

Sometimes it is good to blend several techniques together to make a rose. The blended tea rose is the most beautiful ribbon rose of all the petalled roses. Try this exercise to test your skills in rolled corner petal-making. Here's the challenge: Make a stemmed rose with three leaves, using the four-petal u-gather, the single u-gather, and the rolled corner petal techniques. The prairie point technique will be used for the leaf.

Referring to diagrams 5 and 6 on page 58, use 15 double-headed stamens in a mix of red, yellow, gold, and green, and make a stemmed stamen center for the rose. Use a 5" piece of 20-gauge wire for the stem.

Using the ribbon widths and lengths below, make the petals. Group the petals according to their row number.

Row 1: One four-petal u-gather (8½" of peach/cream ombre wire-edge ribbon, 1" wide). Refer to technique diagrams 70 and 71, page 119.

YOU WILL NEED
1 yd. peachy pink to cream ombre wire-edge ribbon, 1" wide, for the two center rows of the rose
2¼ yd. cream wire-edge ribbon, 1½" wide, for the remaining petals (You may have leftovers, so make buds!).
13½" olive green ombre wire-edge ribbon, 1½" wide, for the leaves and tube calyx
1 yd. olive green bias-cut silk ribbon, ⅝" wide
15 double-headed stamens
5" of wire, 20-gauge
9" of wire, 32-gauge

Row 2: Four single u-gather petals (3½" of peach/cream ombre ribbon, 1" wide). For taller petals, use 4" of 1½" wide ribbon. Refer to technique diagrams 40 and 43, pages 103 and 104.

Row 3: Five rolled corner petals (3½" of cream ribbon, 1½" wide). Refer to technique diagrams 100 through 106, pages 138 and 139 for this row of petals and also for Row 4 and 5.

Row 4: Six rolled corner petals (4" of cream ribbon, 1½" wide)

Row 5: Seven rolled corner petals (4½" of cream ribbon, 1½" wide)

Working clockwise, stitch the first row of petals tightly to the stamen center. Stitch the other petals to this center base in row order. The petals will overlap each other. From time to time, stitch through all the layers of ribbon at the base and pull the thread tightly.

When the rose is complete, cover the back of the rose with a tube calyx. Refer to diagrams 9 and 10, page 61. Wrap the stem with green bias-cut silk ribbon.

Make three stemmed leaves using a 3½" piece of green wired ribbon, 1½" wide for each leaf, and the Prairie Point technique, diagrams 118 to 121, page 153. Use 3" of 32-gauge wire for each leaf stem.

Display the rose in a bud vase, on a hat, as a single flower in a tussy mussy (a Victorian posy holder), or use the flower un-stemmed in a composition of large flowers for a cushion or wall hanging.

Pinch Petal

Pinch petals are a vintage petal technique used to make very simple flowers. The petal is especially good to use for five-petal wild roses and even full-blown roses.

The corsage shown in the photo was made with three different ribbons for the rose and three different greens for the leaves. The stems are wrapped in metallic thread. While this full-blown rose was made with very striking ribbon colors, the rose you make can be any color. Make an easy five-petal rose first and then try the larger full-blown rose. A pink/white five-petal rose is used in the project on page 195.

The petal can be made with the pinch being either at the half-way point in the ribbon length or slightly back from the half-way point.

Pinch Petals Ribbon Guide

Use wire edge ribbon for this technique.

1" wide ribbon—use 2½" to 3" length for each petal

1½" wide ribbon—use 4" to 4½" length for each petal

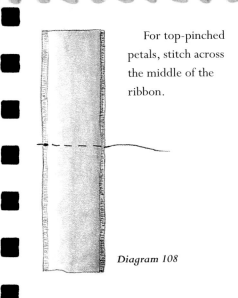

For top-pinched petals, stitch across the middle of the ribbon.

Diagram 108

Gather the ribbon tightly. In some cases, one wrap around the stitching will really cinch in the gathering.

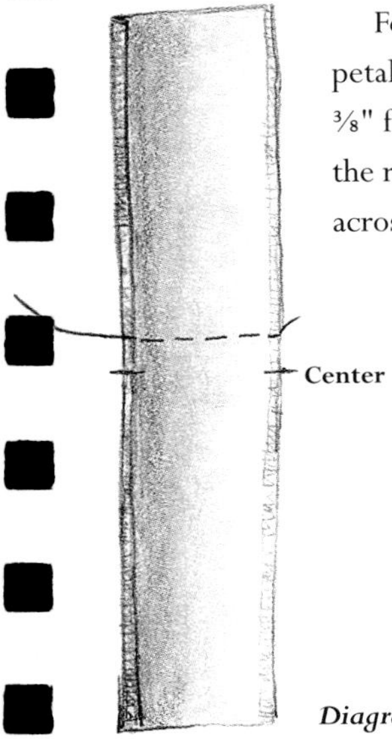

Diagram 110

For back-pinched petals, mark the ribbon ⅜" from the center of the ribbon and stitch across the ribbon.

Center

Diagram 109

For both top- and back-pinched petals, fold the ribbon in half. Narrow the base of the ribbon by tightly gathering it about ³⁄₁₆" from the raw edges.

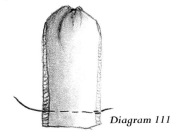

Diagram 111

Finished front view of top-
pinched petal.

Diagram 112

Finished back view of back-
pinched petal.

Diagram 113

Finished Wild Rose with back-pinched petals

Note: When using these petals with a stamen
center, whether the stamens are on a wire stem or
not, stitch the first petal to the stamens and then
evenly arrange the remaining petals in a clockwise
pattern until one row of petals is formed. They
may overlap. If the flower has no stem, coil the
stamen ends on themselves in the back of the
flower and secure with stitches. Or, leave the stamen
stems long and hide them under another flower or
leaf, in a composition.

Diagram 114

Gothic Arch Petal

This petal is fully sewn around the top of the ribbon fold to make the petal shape. It can be hand sewn or machine sewn. This technique is really good to use for a tulip petal, or any other large flower that has slightly arched petals. Use 1½" wide wire-edge ribbon or bias-cut silk ribbon in ribbon lengths of about 5" per petal.

Fold the ribbon in half and sew, with small stitches, the stitch pattern shown. Start the stitching about ¾" from the fold.

Turn the ribbon right-side out and press it flat. Gather the ribbon across the bottom of the petal and pull tightly.

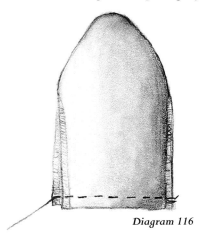

Diagram 116

The finished petal is now ready to be sewn or glued to stemmed stamens.

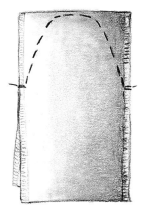

Diagram 115

Diagram 117

Exercise:

Make a vase full of colorful tulips and leaves for your kitchen table.

STEPS:

A tulip has six petals, three stamens, and long, fat leaves.

1. Make a tulip using 30" of 1½" wide wire-edge ribbon in any color. Each petal uses 5" of ribbon.

2. Prepare three black stemmed stamens using 10" of 18-gauge wire. Refer to diagrams 5 and 6 on page 58.

3. Sew or glue the first petal to the stamen center. Arrange and attach two more petals around the stamen center to complete the first row. If using glue, it will help to stabilize the stamens and the stem. Sew (or glue) three more petals in between the first row of petals so they peek out.

4. Cover the raw edges of the petals and the stem with 4" of olive green bias-cut silk ribbon, ⅝" wide.

YOU WILL NEED
30" wire-edge ribbon, 1½" wide
4" olive green bias-cut silk ribbon, ⅝" wide
8" olive green bias-cut silk ribbon, 1½" wide
18" olive green ombre ribbon, 1½" wide
3 stamens
10" of wire, 18-gauge
10" of wire, 22-gauge
White glue or hot glue

5. Make a stem tube cover using 8" of 1½" wide olive green bias-cut silk ribbon. Refer to diagram 11, page 64. Slip it over the stem and glue or stitch it as close to the base of the petals as possible.

6. Make a wide tulip leaf using 18" of olive green ombre ribbon and 10" of 22-gauge wire. Refer to diagram 141, page 165. Cover the raw edges with floral tape.

Arrange the flowers and leaves in a tall vase.

Chapter 9

Techniques:

Leaves

The leaves in this chapter include: prairie point, half-round, curved leaf, boat leaf, half-boat leaf, mitered leaf, and gothic arch leaf. When the leaves are used in a composition, they are usually overlapped with other leaves or flowers so the raw edges at the base of the leaf don't show.

You will make a lot of leaves in ribbonwork. Making up a "Bag-o-Leaves" using a variety of ribbon colors, styles, and sizes will give you plenty of leaves to use in your next flower composition.

As you're looking at the photos in this leaf section, you'll notice that not all leaves are green. Some are ombre blue/green and lavender/green and yet others are metallic. Try some brown, plum, orange, gold, and even lime green leaves and see how these make your flower compositions come to life.

LEFT: Simple, yet elegant ribbon leaves make a stunning embellishment on this purse. The leaves use the prairie point and boat leaf techniques.

Prairie Point

The prairie point leaf is one of the most versatile leaves to use in ribbonwork because it has two sides that are useable. A choice of ombre ribbons further optimizes this technique because you can choose which ribbon color edge will be at the point of the leaf. In all, there are four different results for the same piece of ribbon!

While wire-edge ribbon works best for this technique, feel free to try non-wired styles such as double-faced silk-satin or velvet.

Prairie Point Ribbon Guide

Use wire-edge ribbon as follows:
5/8" wide ribbon—use 2" length
1" wide ribbon—use 2½" length
1½" wide ribbon—use 3½" to 4" length
2" wide ribbon—use 5" length

Tip: *If you only have 1½" wide ribbon on hand and you need to have a slightly smaller leaf, simply stitch higher up from the base of the triangle.*

The first row shows prairie point leaves made from 2" wide ribbon, 1½" wide, 1" wide, and 5/8" wide. In the second row, the first two leaves illustrate ribbon color edge changes as viewed from the front and back. The larger leaves show the front and back with no ribbon color edge change.

If the ribbon is wired, remove the bottom wire. Mark the halfway point of the ribbon length and fold down one end of the ribbon at that point.

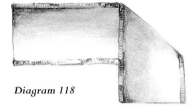

Diagram 118

Fold the other half of the ribbon down.

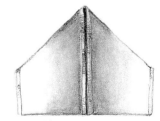

Diagram 119

Tip: *Look at the ribbon on the back side and use the bottom of the "triangle"(bottom edge of the ribbon) as a guide to stitch on. If making a smaller leaf from wide ribbon, sew ¼" up from this base edge.*

Gather across the bottom going through all layers of ribbon. If you're stemming the leaf, add 3" of 32-gauge wire between the ribbon layers at the stitch line.

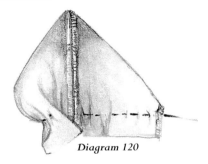

Diagram 120

Gather the stitching very tightly, wrap your thread around the base of the leaf once, pull tightly, and secure the wrap with a few stitches. Cut the thread and trim the excess ribbon from the base of the leaf. If the leaf was stemmed, cover it with bias-cut silk ribbon or floral tape, as discussed on page 63.

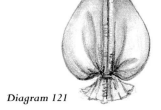

Diagram 121

Half-Round Leaf

It's important to have a variety of leaf shapes in your ribbonwork, and the half-round leaf technique offers that variety. Use small ribbon widths for the small flower compositions and the 1" and 1½" wide ribbons for the large flowers. Ribbons that have interesting textures or edges work well for this technique, as does wire-edge ribbon.

This leaf is best as a small filler leaf; however, it can be used in its large version for a stemmed hollyhock leaf or any large flower that has a round style leaf.

You'll recognize this stitch pattern from the u-gather chapter of the book where it's used to make petals and rosettes. Sew the stitch pattern shown, pull the gathering tightly, and secure it. Trim the excess ribbon from each end.

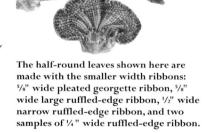

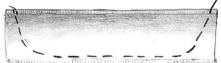

Diagram 122

The half-round leaves shown here are made with the smaller width ribbons: ⅝" wide pleated georgette ribbon, ⅝" wide large ruffled-edge ribbon, ½" wide narrow ruffled-edge ribbon, and two samples of ¼" wide ruffled-edge ribbon.

Half-Round Leaf Ribbon Guide

Use any style of ribbon as follows:

¼" wide ribbon—use 1" length	1" wide ribbon—use 2½" to 4" length
½" to ⅝" wide ribbon—use 1¾" to 2" length	1½" wide ribbon—use 4" to 8" length

Curved Leaf

This is a classic vintage leaf technique that was used time and time again. Because of the simple stitch pattern, this technique lends itself best to the narrower width ribbons; however, a large leaf can be made with

As shown, the selection of ribbons that can be used for the curved leaf technique is quite broad. From top to bottom is 1" wide olive wire-edge ribbon with a stem, 1" wide olive ombre wire-edge, ⅝" wide double-faced silk-satin, ⅜" wide double-faced silk-satin, two samples of ¼" wide ombre ruffled-edge ribbon, and two samples of ¼" wide ombre picot-edge ribbon with the colors reversed.

1½" wide ribbon if desired. Use the leaf in small compositions or as fillers in a slightly larger composition.

Ombre ribbons work well with this technique because they offer you a choice of edge color.

If using an ombre ribbon decide which color edge you want the leaf to have. The color edge you choose will be opposite the stitch pattern. If the ribbon has a ruffled edge, this also will be opposite the stitch pattern.

If the ribbon is wired, remove the wire along the side that will be stitched.

Fold the ribbon in half. Stitch the curved pattern shown, starting at the fold end of the ribbon. The point of the leaf always turns out best when you start your stitching at the fold.

Diagram 123

Pull the stitching thread just until the gathering appears to be in a straight line. The top of the ribbon will now be curved! Do not secure the gathering yet.

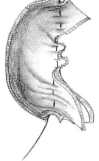

Diagram 124

Open the leaf and adjust the gathering to the shape and fullness of leaf desired. Secure the gathering.

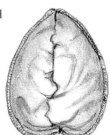

Diagram 125

Flatten the tab (at the point of the leaf) on the back and secure with a stitch. Trim the excess ribbon from the bottom of the leaf. If you're stemming a leaf, whipstitch a 2" to 3" piece of 32-gauge wire along the spine on the back of the leaf. Cover the stem with bias-cut silk ribbon, thread, or floral tape as shown on page 62. The very small leaves are not usually stemmed.

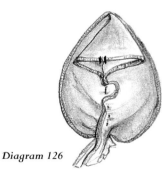

Diagram 126

Curved Leaf Ribbon Guide

Use any style of ribbon as follows:

¼" wide ribbon—use 1¾" to 2" length
⅜" wide ribbon—use 2" to 2¼" length
⅝" wide ribbon—use 4" to 6" length

1" wide ribbon—use 6" to 8" length
1½" wide ribbon—use 10" length

Boat Leaf

This technique has been used for quite some time and is one of the most basic leaves for modern day ribbonwork. Its name is derived from the shape of the ribbon just before it is gathered—it looks like a small paper boat.

Like the curved leaf, the boat leaf gives you a choice of edge color, and the larger versions of the leaf can be stemmed.

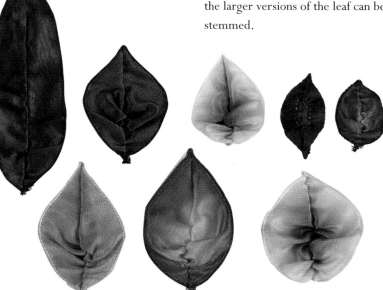

Boat Leaf Ribbon Guide

Use any style of ribbon as follows:
- ⅝" wide ribbon—use 4" to 8" length
- 1" wide ribbon—use 5" to 9" length
- 1½" wide ribbon—use 10" to 13" length

Starting at the left, you'll see a very long boat leaf made from ⅝" wide wired ribbon, using 8" of ribbon. The top row shows a solid green wire-edge ribbon and an ombre wire-edge ribbon both 1" wide. The next leaf is made of ⅝" wide ruffled-edge ribbon, and the last leaf in the top row is of ⅝" wide wire-edge ribbon. For the bottom row of boat leaves, 1" wide ribbon and a variety of edge color and degrees of gathering were used.

Not only leaves can be made with this technique; a lily project is on page 184, while the poinsettia in the photo is made using eight large yellow stamens and a variety of 1" wide red ribbons. There are five medium petals and four large petals. The three green leaves use 1½" wide ribbon. Each of the poinsettia petals and leaves is stemmed with 22-gauge wire and wrapped with green thread (bias-cut silk ribbon works well too), and then combined into a bundle to form a flower. Try your hand at making one of these flowers using this photo and the ribbon length guide on page 157.

Decide which color edge you want the leaf to have and orient it to the diagram shown here. If the ribbon is wired, remove the bottom wire. Fold the ribbon in half.

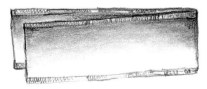

Diagram 127

Turn up the bottom corners of the ribbon so a "boat" shape is formed. The fold end is the tip of the leaf. Begin stitching the pattern from the folded point, on the right, continuing along the edge of the ribbon to the other point.

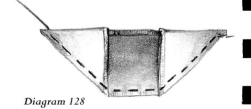

Diagram 128

Pull the gathering thread so the bottom of the "boat" goes straight. Don't secure the gathering yet.

Diagram 129

Open the ribbon and test the gathering until the leaf is the shape you want. Secure the gathering with stitches. Trim off the triangular ribbon tabs at the back of the leaf.

Diagram 130

If stemming a leaf, lay the wire on the back of the leaf and whipstitch it to the spine of the leaf. Cover the stem wire with bias-cut silk ribbon or floral tape.

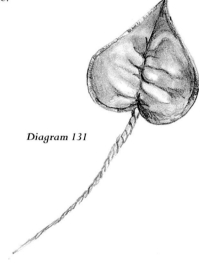

Diagram 131

Half-Boat Leaf

This leaf was developed from the full boat leaf to accommodate smaller ribbon widths. In essence, you just make one-half of a boat leaf. The ribbon widths suitable for this technique are listed on this page and, while you can make a leaf using ¼" wide ribbon, it is easier to use the curve leaf technique for ribbon widths below ⅝" wide.

Half-Boat Leaf Ribbon Guide

Use any style of ribbon as follows:
¼" wide ribbon—use 1¾" to 2¼" length
³/₈" wide ribbon—use 2½" length
½" wide ribbon—use 2¾" length
⅝" wide ribbon—use 3" length
¾" wide ribbon—use 3" length
1" wide ribbon—use 4" length

The half-boat leaves shown were made from ⅝" wide double-faced silk-satin, ½" wide metallic ribbon, ⅜" wide double-faced silk-satin, ⅛" wide ruffled-edge ribbon. The last two leaves were made from ¼" wide ruffled-edge ribbons.

If the ribbon has a ruffled edge, you will be stitching along the straight side. If the ribbon is wired, remove the wire along the side that is stitched. Fold the ribbon in half.

Diagram 132

Turn down the corner on the folded end of the ribbon and stitch the pattern shown. The folded end will be the point of the leaf. Compare this diagram to boat leaf diagram 128 and note the *half* boat shape of the ribbon.

Diagram 133

Slightly gather the ribbon and secure the gathering with backstitches. Open the ribbon and gather across the bottom edge.

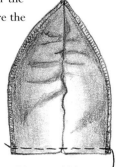

Diagram 134

Gather the stitches tightly and secure. Trim the tails of the leaf.

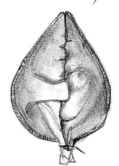

Diagram 135

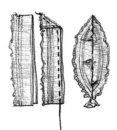

Diagram 136

This group of illustrations shows the half-boat technique using narrow ribbons.

Mitered Leaf

This is an excellent leaf to use if it's openly exposed in a composition with nothing to overlap it, for example, a leaf on a vine. The way it's made allows for the raw end at the bottom to be turned up in the back and still keep a nice petal shape. This leaf also will give you a choice of ribbon edge color if using ombre ribbons.

As the photo shows, there are no raw edges when making mitered leaves. The ribbons used here are 1½" wide olive wire-edge, two samples of 1" wide ombre wire-edge showing edge color changes, and 1" wide lime wire-edge. Depending on the length of ribbon used, you'll get variations in the gathered section of the leaf.

Mitered Leaf Ribbon Guide

Use wire-edge ribbon:
　　1" wide ribbon—use 3" to 3¾" length
　　1½" wide ribbon—use 4½" to 5¼" length

If using ombre ribbon, decide which color will be on the outside edge of the leaf. Fold the ribbon in half. The ribbon length you use may, or may not, look like the diagram.

Diagram 137

Fold down the corner on the folded edge of the ribbon. Stitch a seam along the diagonal, sewing through all four layers of ribbon. Secure the stitching and cut off the thread.

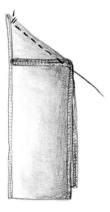

Diagram 138

Open the ribbon. Stitch across the ribbon as shown. Sometimes this may be a slightly scooped stitch pattern depending on the length of ribbon used.

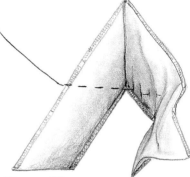

Diagram 139

Gather the stitching tightly and secure with backstitches. The leaf will be slightly puffed out on the front side. Trim the ends from the base of the leaf and tuck the tails under.

Diagram 140

Gothic Arch

Depending on the width of ribbon used the leaves can be quite skinny or rather fat. The leaves can be used as large fillers for a group of flowers in a vase, or they can be flower specific, such as for use with lilies, tulips, jonquils, and daffodils.

Gothic Arch Ribbon Guide

Use wire-edge ribbon and a length of 22-gauge wire the same length as the ribbon:

⅝" wide ribbon—use 9" to 12" length for a small leaf

1" wide ribbon—use 12" to 18" length for a medium leaf

1½" wide ribbon—use 18" length for a large leaf

Fold the ribbon in half and stitch the pattern shown. Start stitching at the edge, 2" to 3" down from the fold.

Turn the ribbon right-side out and press flat. Make a "hook" at one end of the wire and insert the wire into the ribbon cavity. Secure the raw edge at the base of the ribbon with a dot of glue.

Fold a small pleat at the base of the ribbon and secure the ribbon to the wire with floral tape. The remaining stem wire can be cut off once you've determined the length needed for the arrangement.

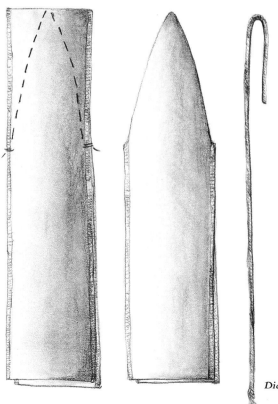

Diagram 141

Chapter 10

Bits and Pieces, Odds and Ends

This is the chapter that contains odd bits of information. You'll learn something about dying ribbons, making bases and dresses for half dolls, covering cardboard with fabric, and mixing ribbon techniques to create flowers.

LEFT: A small footstool pincushion with a fabulous mix of ribbon flowers created from a wide variety of ribbons and techniques.

Ribbons and laces have been hand painted with dyes. Sometimes the flowers were made first and then dyed; other times the ribbon was dyed first and then made into flowers.

How to Dye Ribbons

Dying ribbon is all about experimentation, so don't be afraid to give it a go. At the very worst, you'll have a color of ribbon you don't like, and then again you just might discover something fabulous!

Buy a selection of white ribbons (silk and rayon work well) in a variety of weaves: straight-weave, bias-cut, double-faced ribbons. In addition to the double-faced and rayon ribbons, use silk embroidery ribbons, in widths of ⅛", ¼", ½", and 1¼".

Some rayon lace appliqués and rayon fringing, as used to make half doll tassels, can also be dyed successfully, so have some of these on hand.

You'll also need dyes; find one that works well on silks and in a range of basic primary and secondary colors. It's more fun to mix your own colors! Buy an artist's color wheel; it's useful for learning about color mixing.

Have on hand two containers for water, several small cups for the dyes, a small measuring cup, an eyedropper, several large and small round brushes, some latex gloves, paper towels, and tongs for lifting the ribbon out of the dye bath.

Preparation Steps:

1. Cover the table surface with a plastic cloth.

2. Set up two containers of clear water—one to clean your brush and one to pre-wet your ribbon.

3. Put a small amount of each concentrated dye color into small, separate containers.

4. Mix the dyes to the strength you prefer, or as recommended by the dye manufacturer. Start with this *very rough* guideline: Make a medium wash of each dye color by adding 5 drops of dye to ⅓ cup of water in a large cup/container. Make a light wash of each dye color by adding ⅓ cup of medium wash mix to ⅓ cup of water. Add more concentrated dye or water as needed.

Pre-wet the ribbon just prior to dying the ribbon.

White paper towels are handy for testing color, cleaning your brush, and laying the wet ribbon on.

Dip Dying Technique:

Dip the ribbon into the lightest wash of dye. Stir continuously for even dying. The longer the ribbon is left in the dye bath, the stronger the color will be. Remove the ribbon when the desired color is achieved, usually between 30 seconds and 2 minutes, following the recommendation of the dye manufacturer.

Edge Dyed Technique:

Wet the ribbon in clear water, then remove it and lay it on a paper towel. Brush on color to one edge of the wet ribbon. Or, roll up the ribbon and dip one end of it in the dye bath.

Brushed Wet-Into-Wet Technique:

Pre-dye ribbon to the desired color. Lay the wet ribbon on a paper towel. While the ribbon is still wet, brush on some other colors of dye in a random manner.

Graduated Dying Technique:

Dip the ribbon or fringing in the lightest wash, then dip part of the ribbon or fringing in the next darkest wash. Lay out the ribbon or fringing on a paper towel to dry. When dry, carefully iron the ribbon and shake out the fringing.

Pre-Made Ribbon Flowers Technique:

Sew a selection of ribbon flowers using the instructions in this book and the various white silk ribbons you have. Pre-wet a flower, then brush on the lightest color of dye in the area you want it. Darken or shade the flower with the next darker color or another color of dye. This was a very popular technique during the 1920s and was a way to give a rather bland ribbon color a bit more depth.

Half Doll Underpinnings and a Dress Pattern

Have you ever wondered what was under an antique half doll? Sometimes it was a metal frame, a pincushion, a lamp, or even a box. With your old half doll inherited from Granny or with a new reproduction half doll, it's easy to make a base and a dress for your doll using some of the ideas presented here.

This 3" tall half doll sits atop a mahogany box. She is sewn to a miniature pincushion base—like a little tuffet or a small squashed tomato—and her legs are stitched to the side of this tuffet so she gives an impression of being seated. The dress is made from two rows of 1¼" wide silk ribbon gathered and stitched to a circle of fabric. The ribbon coil roses are made from ¼" wide ribbon.

Make a Pincushion for a Half Doll

Method 1:

The very simplest pincushion base is a ball shape. Using a circle of muslin, sew around the edge of the circle and draw it up. Before tightening the gathering, pack the cavity tightly with pillow stuffing. Once the cavity is packed, tighten the gathering and secure with backstitches. Without cutting the thread, sew the doll through the sew holes at the waist, to the top of the ball.

Pincushion Bases for Half Dolls (round)

Cut muslin circles of the following diameters to create pincushion bases for half dolls.

> 10" diameter—2" to 2½" tall half doll
> 16" diameter—3" to 3½" tall half doll
> 21" diameter—3¾" tall half doll.

Method 2:

Another pincushion base can be made from a rectangle of muslin sewn into a tube shape with a fabric circle sewn onto the base of the tube, diagram 142. Use ½" seam allowances. A small cardboard circle (cut to fit inside the tube), slipped into the base of the muslin tube before the tube is packed with pillow stuffing, will help stabilize the pincushion. Gather around the top of the tube about ½" to 1" from the edge of the fabric. Tighten and secure the thread after the tube is tightly packed with pillow stuffing, diagram 143. Sew the half doll to the top of the tube.

Pincushion Bases for Half Dolls (tube-shaped)

Cut muslin pieces of the following dimensions to create a tube-shaped pincushion base for a half doll.

> 11" x 5" rectangle and a 4" fabric circle—2" to 2½" tall doll
> 13" x 7" rectangle and a 4¾" circle—3" to 3½" half doll
> 13" x 9" rectangle and a 4¾" circle—3¾" tall half doll

Diagram 142

Diagram 143

Wire Frame: If you're not using a pincushion underneath your half doll, consider a wire frame, similar to diagram 144. A lampshade frame will work too, as long as it has enough wire support at the top. Thread a piece of 32-gauge wire through each sew hole on the half doll. Continue threading that wire through a corresponding hole in a matte board circle directly under the doll's body. Set the doll/ cardboard on the wire stand and twist each of the wires down and around the nearest frame leg or supporting wire. A pair of needle nose pliers is helpful for tightening the wires. WARNING: Be very careful not to crack the porcelain doll base.

Diagram 144

Two Simple Skirt Patterns for a Half Doll
Method 1: Tube Skirt

To make a very simple tube skirt for your half doll, use 18" to 30" of fabric, 4" to 7" wide. The length and width of the fabric will depend on the half doll size and the size of pincushion the dress is covering. Sew the rectangle of fabric into a tube shape. Turn up a ¼" hem at the bottom. Gather the top edge of the tube and slip it over the doll's head. Tighten and secure the gathering. Cover the waist with a piece of ribbon—ruched ⅜" wide satin ribbon is very pretty. In a few places near the waist area, tack the dress to the pincushion base. Decorate the dress with ribbon flowers and bows and add a little silver chatelaine at the waist.

Method 2: Panel Skirt

A fabric four-panel skirt is a good choice when you don't want a lot of gathered fabric around the doll's waist. The pattern in diagram 145 can be increased 150% so it fits a small 2½" doll or 200% so it fits a larger 3¾" doll, such as the "Melinda" half doll project on page 241. Experiment with the pattern. Add or take a little off the sides, shorten or lengthen it until you get a custom fit for your doll. This skirt can be a single layer skirt with a hem if you use four panels of fabric or it can be padded and self-lined if you cut eight pieces of fabric. Use ¼" seams.

To construct a single layer skirt, sew four panels together at the long seams so a tapered cone shape is formed. Turn up the hem.

To construct the padded, self-lined skirt, sew as you did for the single layer skirt, omitting the hem. For the lining, sew ¼" loft batting to the other four fabric panels before sewing them together; don't forget to leave a 2" opening. With right sides together and the seam openings aligned, sew the padded lining to the outer skirt at the hemline (¼" seam). Turn the fabric right sides out. Press the fabric and sew a tacking stitch around the top of the skirt to hold the fabric layers together. Decorate the skirt at the hemline, adding flowers and an optional pocket. Slip the decorated

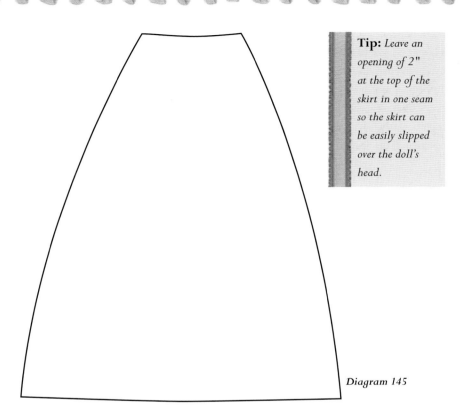

Tip: *Leave an opening of 2" at the top of the skirt in one seam so the skirt can be easily slipped over the doll's head.*

Diagram 145

skirt over the doll's head. Sew up the 2" gap in the seam. Tighten the waist area with gathering stitches as needed and cover the waist with a length of ribbon.

To make a self-lined apron for your skirt, cut two skirt panels and sew them together at the side seams. If you're adding a lace overlay to the apron, sandwich the lace between the fabric before you sew up the side seams. Turn the apron right-side out. Leave the apron open at the top and bottom until you have finished decorating it with ribbon flowers, and then sew it closed. A 12" length of ⅜" wide ribbon sewn to the top of the apron allows you to tie it around the doll's waist.

Use this pattern at this size for a small pocket or enlarge it 200% for a larger pocket like the one on the "Melinda" half doll project, page 240. To make a self-lined pocket for your doll's skirt, sew two pieces of fabric together using ¼" seams. Leave an opening in the seam and turn right-side out. Press the fabric, smoothing out the curves. Sew the seam opening closed. Fold the pocket up by a third and fold the curved flap down. Sew the side seams together to form a pocket. Decorate the pocket with ribbons, trims, and flowers. Sew the pocket to the skirt.

Diagram 146

Covering Cardboard with Fabric

A Rectangle with Mitered Corners

When covering a piece of square-cornered cardboard, make very neat, mitered corners. Fold over and glue each long edge of fabric to the back of the board. Fold under the short end corners in a miter and glue to the back of the board. Think of wrapping a present, except the miter will be much smaller. The small Halloween "Hang-Up" has the dark gold background fabric folded with mitered corners and, because the back of the covered board was to be seen from the front, the miters had to be very, very neat. Small peacock breast feathers were placed at the corners as a design element. However, this is a good trick if there is a mistake with your mitering!

Using a homemade fabric print, some gold silk fabric, small trims, and bits and pieces from the ribbon stash, a seasonal ornament such as this can be made. Only one ribbon rosette was made and used in this design.

Diagram 147

A Circle

The amount of fabric that you need to cover a cardboard circle should be 1½" larger than the diameter of the cardboard. Sometimes you will pad the cardboard with some batting before covering it with fabric. Sew with double thread. Start your stitching ¼" in from the edge of the fabric. Run gathering stitches around the circle then place the cardboard circle in the center of the fabric. Pull the gathering tightly, adjusting the fabric as needed for a smooth fit, and secure the gathering with back stitches. A few "laced" stitches across the back keep the fabric stretched tightly.

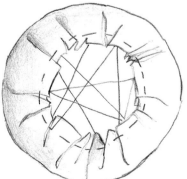

Diagram 148

A 2" circle of cardboard is covered in silk fabric and then filled with folded roses and turned into a pendant. A felt backing covers the raw side of the covered circle.

Combining Ribbon Techniques

Combining ribbonwork techniques will often result in some wonderful flowers and in particular, roses. Look carefully at Chapter 12, *More Challenging Projects*, and see how many combination flowers you can spot.

Here are a few flower recipes using the techniques in this book:

Fantasy Rose - a folded rose center with a u-gather ruffle

Fantasy Rose - a coiled rose center with five-petal zigzag ruching

Tea Rose - a folded rose center with three, five, or seven u-gather petals

Tea Rose - a folded rose center with five, seven, or nine rolled corner petals

Tea Rose - a coiled rose center with three to eleven rolled corner petals

Cabochon Rose - a folded rose center with two rows of three u-gather petals

Cabochon Rose - a folded rose center with three, four, or five rolled-edge u-gather petals

Cabochon Rose - a coiled rose center with three or five u-gather petals

Cabochon Rose - a coiled rose center with three u-gather petals and five outer u-gather petals

Wild Rose - a twisted spiral center with twisted petals, a five-petal u-gather, or five dipped corner petals

Pansy and Violet - two petal continuous u-gather back and a three-petal continuous u-gather front

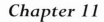

Chapter 11

Easy Projects

*Now that you have practiced a
few of the ribbonwork techniques,
you are ready to tackle a
project or two. The projects in
this chapter are easy and will
give you much pleasure. Read
each project through before
you begin and then enjoy
the process of creating
something beautiful.*

"Leigh" Powder Patter

The powder patters in this group are from the 1920s, except the plum one with the porcelain bas-relief head which is new. The backs were decorated with ribbon flowers and the handles, not seen, were wrapped in ribbon.

Steps:

1. Make one vintage flat rose using 6" of dusty pink/gold ribbon and a ¾" circle of crinoline. Refer to diagrams 82 through 86 on pages 129 and 130.

2. Make one blue/red double rosette using 2½" of ribbon and a blue bead center. Fold the ribbon up two-thirds and sew the variation u-gather technique, diagrams 52 through 54 on page 109.

3. Make two purple/yellow rosettes using 2½" of ribbon, one gold seed bead per rosette, and the u-gather technique, diagrams 40 through 42 on page 103.

4. Make four green/yellow curved leaves using 2" of ribbon per leaf and the curved leaf technique, diagrams 123 through 126 on pages 155 and 156.

5. Sew the gold net, or old lace, over the silk fabric circle.

6. Sew the porcelain head to the center of the silk fabric circle. Ruche the wine suede ribbon and sew it to the base of the porcelain head neckline.

7. Sew the dusty pink/gold rose to the center of the neckline. Add a purple rosette on each side and two leaves. Sew the green loop leaf trim under the flowers. Sew on beads. Sew the blue/red double rosette and two leaves above the doll's head.

8. Glue the padding to the cardboard circle. Cover the padded cardboard with fabric. Review diagram 148 on page 178. Gather the silk fabric circle and place it over the padded cardboard circle. Pull tightly and smooth out fabric. Sew green/lavender trim around the outer edge of the circle. Fold the 27" of plum fabric in half so it is 1" wide. Gather it to fit around the padded fabric circle. Glue the ruffle in place with white glue. Set aside.

9. Glue the dowel stick to the back of the powder puff and secure with stitches along the stick's length. Very lightly glue, then wrap the dowel stick with 22" of dark gold ribbon starting at the end of the stick and working toward the powder

Makeup and beauty items were very much in vogue during the 1920s and thus many manufacturers catered to milady and her needs with a multitude of dainty accessories. One of those was the powder patter—a powder puff, attached to a stick and embellished with ribbons, flowers, bas-relief heads, and trims. Sometimes, a matching mirror was also available.

You will need:

"Leigh" sew-on flat back porcelain half doll head
3¾" powder puff
3¾" cardboard circle
4" circle of batting, ¼" thick
5" circle of vintage gold net or old lace
5" fabric circle of plum dupioni silk
27" x 2" piece of plum dupioni silk
12" dowel stick, ¼" thick
22" dark gold ribbon to cover handle
10" of above ribbon for bow
1¾" vintage metallic tassel
13" lavender/green loop trim
4" wine suede ribbon, ⅜" wide
4" of green loop leaf trim
6" dusty pink/gold wire-edge ribbon, ⅝" wide
2½" blue/red ribbon, ⅝" wide
4 ½" purple/yellow ruffled-edge ribbon, ¼" wide
8" yellow/green ruffled-edge ribbon, ¼" wide
¾" circle of crinoline
White glue

puff. Glue the tassel to the end of the stick. Cover the end of the stick with a tied bow that covers the cord ends of the tassel.

10. Glue the decorated fabric back to the wrong side of the powder puff covering the stick. Hold with clothespins to dry. DO NOT put weights on the porcelain head.

A lily spray in a simple vase is very striking. When used on a hat, a lily with beaded petals is very elegant. This is a very easy flower to do and is based on the boat leaf technique.

You will need:

60" pink/white wire-edge ribbon, 1" wide

3" wire, 32-gauge

6" wire, 22-gauge

6 wine-colored lily stamens

Floral tape

Hot glue

Lily

LEFT: A group of ribbon lilies and hydrangea assembled atop an old music cabinet makes a lovely arrangement.

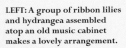

Steps:

A lily has six petals and six stamens.

1. Secure six wine lily stamens together with a 3" piece of 32-gauge wire. Hot glue this to a 6" piece of 22-gauge wire.

2. Do not remove any wires from the ribbon. Fold one 10" piece of wired ribbon in half across its width and use the boat leaf technique, diagrams 127 through 131 on pages 158 and 159. Trim off the ribbon tabs at the back of the petal.

3. Make five more petals.

4. Assemble the lily by stitching or gluing three of the petals around the stamen center. Attach the other three petals in between the first petals. Finish the lily stem with floral tape or bias-cut silk ribbon.

5. Several lilies can be joined together on a single stem— just as in nature—and placed in a vase.

Sachets with Blossom Flowers

Ribbonwork doesn't get much simpler than this project! Three blossoms and a few leaves decorate the front of a sweet little ribbon sachet. Or, use a flapper head as the centerpiece of the composition and surround her with blossoms. Either way is reflective of the vintage style of sachets from the 1920s.

You will need:

9" pink ribbon or fabric, 3" wide

7" fine lace, 2" wide

4½" dark pink double-faced silk-satin ribbon, ⅜" wide

4½" dusty pink double-faced silk-satin ribbon, ⅜" wide

4½" pale peach double-faced silk-satin ribbon, ⅜" wide

6" green/yellow ruffled-edge ribbon, ¼" wide

12" cream double-faced silk-satin ribbon, ⅜" wide

2" circle of crinoline

6 yellow double-headed stamens

LEFT: Sachets decorated with ribbon blossoms and leaves can be used for many purposes such as bridal showers, party favors, and teacher gifts. A bas relief flapper head surrounded in silk blossoms is also an idea for the front of the sachet.

Use wide taffeta ribbon, sheer organdy fabric, or dupioni silk fabric. These sachets are filled with lavender or potpourri and can be used in linen closets, dresser drawers, or even to hang in a powder room.

Steps:

1. Turn under the raw edges of the 3" wide ribbon about ½" and then sew a piece of lace to each end.

2. Fold the ribbon in half with right sides together, aligning the lace tops. Sew up the two side seams, stitching very close to the ribbon edges. Turn right-side out.

3. Make the flowers. Make three blossoms using 4½" each of the pink ribbons. Refer to the four petal u-gather diagrams 70 and 71 on page 119. Gather the ribbon tightly and secure it. Insert two stamens into the center of each blossom, catching the stems with a few stitches at the ribbon center.

4. Make the leaves. Make three curved leaves using 2" of green/yellow ruffled ribbon for each leaf. Refer to the curved leaf diagrams 123 through 126 on pages 155 and 156.

5. Sew the three blossoms to the center of the crinoline. Tuck the three leaves in between the blossoms. Trim away the excess crinoline and tack the flower composition to the front of the sachet.

6. Fill the sachet with lavender or potpourri, and secure the top with a tied shoelace bow using the cream ⅜" wide cream satin ribbon. Trim the tails of the bow.

Purple Hat with Coil Rose

The rose decoration on this hat is the focus of this project. It's not hard to do at all and can be made in one evening! The large rose and the tiny rosettes are both based on the upright coil u-gather technique. The leaves are based on the prairie point technique. This garnishment can be used, not only on hats, but also as a beautiful addition to a coat or the centerpiece on a pillow.

You will need:

36" purple/brown ombre wire-edge ribbon, 1½" wide

13½" purple/red ruffled-edge ribbon, ¼" wide

38½" olive green ombre wire-edge ribbon, 1½" wide

7" red/green wire-edge ribbon, 1½" wide

2" circle of crinoline

5" x 6" rectangle of crinoline

Optional: seed beads and fancy beads.

LEFT: A simple fabric hat can be trimmed with a scrunched piece of silk fabric for a hatband and a sumptuous coil rose for a most sophisticated millinery creation.

Steps:

1. Make the large coil rose using the purple/brown wire-edge ribbon and the upright coil u-gather technique, diagrams 49 through 51 on pages 107 and 108. Make a tight cylinder shape for the center of the rose and sew it to the center of the 2" crinoline circle. Gently gather the ribbon and coil it around the center. The ribbon will be upright. After the rose is made, sew it onto one side of the crinoline rectangle. Set it aside until the leaves have been added.

2. Make eleven prairie point leaves using 3½" of ribbon for each leaf. Make nine leaves, from the olive ombre ribbon—seven using the dark side of the ribbon and two using the light side of the ribbon. Make two red/green leaves. Refer to the prairie point leaf diagrams 118 through 121 on page 153. Sew the leaves to the side of the coil rose on the rectangle of crinoline. The leaves should overlap each other and taper out to a point.

3. Make three tiny coil rosettes using 4½" per rose of the ¼" wide purple/red ruffled ribbon and the upright coil u-gather technique, diagrams 49 through 51 on pages 107 amd 108. Make a tight cylinder shape for the center of the rosette and gently gather the ribbon. Coil the ribbon on itself so an upright rose shape is formed. Secure the coils with stitches. The rosette will be upright. Sew the rosettes over the leaves and the large rose.

4. Finish styling the large rose by slightly flattening it with your hand and tilting the center toward one side. Tack these folds down in a few places as shown in "thread sculpting," diagrams 94 and 95 page 135. The addition of a few fancy beads and seed beads on the petals gives the rose sparkle. More beads on the leaf tips give the suggestion of dewdrops.

5. Cut away the excess crinoline and tack the composition to a hat, pillow, or project of your choice.

Pinecone Ornament with Ribbon Flowers

A pinecone topped with bias-cut silk ribbon roses, a few feathers and a bird might be hard to imagine, but this little beauty holds its own on any holiday tree. Other styles of ribbon can be substituted, of course, as can the decorations - why not try a half doll! For that matter, why not decorate the pinecone so it can be hung up all year!

You will need:

4" pinecone

5" thread-covered wire, 32-gauge

5 yd. red/green bias-cut silk ribbon, 1" wide

45" burgundy bias-cut silk ribbon, 1" wide

10" olive green bias-cut silk cording, ¼" wide

Small mushroom bird

4 small pieces of artificial pine greenery

4 small berry twigs

6 small peacock breast feathers

Hot glue gun and glue

Steps:

1. Make a loop out of the 5" piece of wire and hot glue it onto the top of the pinecone. This is the ring through which to tie the cord hanger.

2. Using the five yards of 1" wide red/green ribbon, begin with one end and glue it to the top of the pinecone. Angle the ribbon downward and loosely drape the ribbon a few inches around the pinecone. Glue the ribbon deeply into a crevice in the pinecone. Repeat this process until the pinecone is loosely decorated with the ribbon. Cut off the remaining ribbon.

3. Make six folded roses using 15" of ribbon for each rose and the folded rose technique, diagrams 87 through 92, pages 132 and 133. Make three roses from the burgundy color and three from the red/green color. Set aside the roses.

4. Glue the artificial greenery to the top of the pinecone, followed by the berry twigs.

5. Glue the roses to the top of the pinecone, in and around the greenery so the raw edges and wire loop are hidden.

6. Glue the small bird to the top of the composition.

7. Glue small peacock feathers in and around the greenery near the top of the pinecone.

8. Make a "tassel" by cutting six 5" pieces of the 1" wide red/green ribbon. Sew the pieces together at one end and glue to the bottom of the pinecone.

9. Tie the 10" piece of green silk cording through the ring.

10. Hang the ornament on a holiday tree, from a cabinet knob, or use on a lampshade key.

Cell Phone Case and Lipstick Pouch

By using small amounts of beautiful jacquard ribbons, a charming cell phone case and lipstick pouch can be made. With the addition of some ribbon flowers, a few beads, and a small tassel, these items are ready for use and won't be missed in any handbag.

You will need:

13" metallic jacquard ribbon (8" pouch, 5" tab closure), 1¾" wide

5" red ribbon to match fabric, 1½" wide

5" chenille-edged ribbon, ½" wide

1 medium-faceted crimson bead

12 crimson seed beads

30 gold seed beads

Large snap closure

2 (8") squares of red dupioni silk fabric

1 (8") square of ¼" thick batting

Sewing machine and red thread

LEFT: Elegant pouches for your cell phone and lipstick are easily made from ribbons. With the addition of a simple ribbon flower the pouches are ready to go.

Cell Phone
Steps:

1. Layer the 8" square of batting and one piece of the silk fabric. Sew around the edges.

2. Topstitch by hand or machine 8" of jacquard ribbon across the center of the other piece of silk fabric.

3. With right sides together sew the two pieces of silk fabric together leaving a 4" opening on one side for turning. See diagram 149.

4. Turn right-side out and sew the opening closed.

5. Fold the fabric square right sides together along the sides with no ribbon. Stitch along this side. This is the back seam of the pouch.

6. Flatten the fabric seam and position it so it is in the center and sew across the bottom of the pouch. Now the pouch is complete. See diagram 150. Turn right-side out.

Diagram 149

Diagram 150

7. Make the chenille-edge rosette using the u-gather technique, diagrams 40 through 42, page 103. Sew the flower to the 5" piece of jacquard ribbon that will be used for the tab closure. Add a red bead center. Secure the outside edges of the flower with gold seed beads.

8. Line the back of the jacquard ribbon tab closure with plain red ribbon. Turn the ribbon ends under and sew around the edges. Stitch the closure to the center back of the pouch.

9. Sew a snap to the inside front of the tab closure, and to the front of the pouch.

Lipstick Pouch
Steps:

1. Thread the ribbon through the mini brass frame until the raw ends of the ribbon are at the bottom on the inside of the pouch. See diagram 151.

2. Sew these inside raw ends together, right sides facing. See diagram 152.

3. Using thread to match the ribbon, sew up the inner side seams of the lining and then the outer seam on the pouch.

4. Make a folded rose with gathered extension using 4½" of gold silk-satin ribbon and refer to the instructions for diagram 93, page 134 .

5. Make a small folded rose using 2½" of gold silk-satin ribbon and the folded rose technique diagrams 87 through 91, pages 132 and 133.

6. Stitch the flowers to the front of the pouch. Sew the yellow rosebud trim around the roses.

7. Decorate a simple thread tassel with a few beads. Attach this tassel to a jump ring and lobster claw jewelry finding. Clip the lobster claw closure on to the purse frame rings. This keeps the purse frame closed.

Diagram 151

Diagram 152

You will need:

18" metallic jacquard ribbon, 1¾" wide

7" gold silk-satin ribbon, ⅜" wide

3" yellow rosebud trim

Mini brass ribbon purse frame

Gold metallic thread tassel

Assorted small red beads

Large lobster claw jewelry finding for closure

White and red thread for hand sewing

Added idea: *String a very narrow piece of silk ribbon through the lobster claw's jump ring closure if you want to have the lipstick case hung as a pendant.*

Mixed Large Roses in a Jardinière

This "project" is an exercise in rose-making using seven techniques. The techniques are: silk coil rose with six-petal extension, folded rose, pinch petal wild rose, dipped corner wild rose, rolled corner tea rose and buds, prairie point leaf, and boat leaf.

You will need:

30" peachy/pink satin silk bias-cut ribbon, 2½" wide

72" cream wire-edge ribbon, 1½" wide

13¾" pink/white ombre wire-edge ribbon, 1" wide

16¼" dusty pink ombre wire-edge ribbon, 1½" wide

81½" raspberry/cinnamon ombre wire-edge ribbon, 1½" wide

17½" olive green ombre wire-edge ribbon, 1½" wide

17½" hunter green ombre wire-edge ribbon, 1½" wide

15" olive green ombre wire-edge ribbon, 1" wide

15" red/green wire-edge ribbon, 1" wide

8" square of crinoline

Steps:

1. Make one peach coiled silk rose using 30" of peachy/pink silk-satin bias-cut ribbon and referring to the top fold coil rose with six continuous petal extensions, diagram 75, page 121. After the cylinder center has been rolled and secured, mark the remaining ribbon into six or seven 4" segments and follow the stitch pattern in the diagram. You may or may not have a small piece of ribbon left over.

2. Make three cream folded roses, referring to the folded rose diagrams 87 through 92, pages 132 and 133. One large rose uses 36" of cream wire-edge ribbon, and the two small roses use 18" each of cream wire-edge ribbon.

3. Make one pink/white wild rose using five 2¾" pieces of pink/white wire-edge ribbon per petal and the pinch petal technique (back pinch), diagrams 109 through 114, pages 145 and 146. Use 10 stamens for the center.

4. Make one dusty pink wild rose using five 3¼" pieces of pink ombre wire-edge ribbon and the dipped corner petal technique, diagrams 96 through 99, pages 136 and 137. Use 15 stamens for the center.

5. Make one large tea rose using 39½" of raspberry/cinnamon wired ribbon. This rose has a folded rose center and two rows of rolled corner petals. Row 1, the center of the rose, uses 9" of ribbon and the folded rose technique diagrams 87 through 92, pages 132 and 133. Row 2 uses five 3" pieces of ribbon and the rolled corner petal technique diagrams 100 through 107, pages 138 and 139. Row 3 uses five 3½" pieces of ribbon and the rolled corner petal technique diagrams 100 through 107, pages 138 and 139.

6. Make one small tea rose using 27" of raspberry/cinnamon wire-edge ribbon and the rolled corner petal technique, diagrams 100 through 107, pages 138 and 139. Make nine petals using 3" of ribbon for each. Overlap and sew three petals together to form the center. Follow this with three more petals evenly arranged to form a second row. The third row has three petals placed between the second row petals. Be sure to keep the tops of the petals even.

7. Make two tea rose buds using 15" of raspberry/cinnamon wire-edge ribbon and the rolled corner petal technique diagrams 100 through 107, pages 138 and 139. Each bud uses 2½" of ribbon per petal. Make three petals for each bud. Roll the first petal on itself and sew the other two petals around it. Repeat for the second bud.

8. Make ten prairie point leaves—five olive green and five dark green. Each leaf uses 3½" of ribbon and the prairie point technique diagrams 118 through 121, page 153.

9. Make six boat leaves—three olive green and three red/green. Each leaf uses 5" of ribbon and the boat leaf technique diagrams 127 through 131, pages 158 and 159.

10. When all the roses and leaves are complete, stitch them to the crinoline in an arrangement that is pleasing to you or use the triangle design shown in the photo. Cut away the excess crinoline and use the composition in a project of your choice.

RIGHT: Reminiscent of a Victorian era color scheme, this vase of mixed ribbon roses on hand-dyed velvet could be framed, or used on an old fashioned photo album.

You will need:

Small tin can (approx. 2⅝" diameter by 3⅛" tall)

Pillow stuffing to fill the tin can

Small spool of heavy thread or dental floss

2½" diameter circle of thin batting

6" diameter circle of thin batting

2¾" x 9" piece of thin batting

2 (6" diameter) circles of pink taffeta fabric

10" pink moiré ribbon or fabric, 3" wide

10" lace, 3" wide

25" pink ruffled edge ribbon, ½" wide

20" pink silk flower bud trim

12" embroidery silk ribbon, ⅝" wide

4½" lavender/pink ruffled-edge ribbon, ¼" wide

6" green/yellow ruffled-edge ribbon, ¼" wide

5 pink bud/stamens

6" medium green silk-satin ribbon, ⅛" wide

1½" x 3" piece of crinoline

6 gold seed beads

White glue

LEFT: Three small tin cans have been converted into pretty pincushions with a rather vintage style about them. One sports a very wide lily of the valley jacquard ribbon, while another uses a smaller jacquard ribbon covered in forget-me-nots. The top decoration for the blue pincushion is lace with an old costume jewelry brooch surrounded by ribbon rosettes. The center pink pincushion with antique lace shows off some sterling silver sewing tools.

Tin Can Pincushion with Ribbon Flowers

A very simple pincushion can be made from a tin can, some fabric, ribbons, laces, and trims. The project described below uses a 3⅛" tall tin can; however, any small-sized tin can will work. This would be a good project to do if you're a beginner because you'll need a pincushion for your ribbonwork!

Steps:

Refer to diagram 153, page 200, as you are assembling the pincushion.

1. Empty the contents of the tin can, then wash and dry it thoroughly. Spray inside and out with a clear sealer. Let it dry.

2. Glue the 2½" circle of thin batting to the bottom of the tin can.

3. Cover the bottom of the can with one of the pink fabric circles. Hold the fabric with a rubber band. Glue the edges of the fabric to the tin can. Secure the fabric with strong thread or dental floss. Remove the rubber band and trim the fabric edges.

4. Stuff the can with pillow stuffing, packing it tightly so a dome shape is formed at the top.

5. Cover the top of the can with a 6" circle of thin batting and the remaining pink circle of fabric. Fasten as you did for the bottom of the can, in step 3.

6. Place and glue the 2¾" x 9" piece of thin batting around the can. Brush on the glue for easier adhesion.

7. Lightly glue the 3" wide ribbon over the batting. Turn under the raw edges of the ribbon at the seam and glue or stitch to secure.

8. Glue the lace over the ribbon at the top and bottom edges. Spot glue the lace using a toothpick in various areas.

9. Glue the pink ruffled-edge ribbon to the top and bottom of the lace edges. Glue the pink silk flower bud trim over the ruffled ribbon.

10. Make one pink coil rose using 5" of the ½" wide pink ruffled-edge ribbon and the upright coil u-gather diagrams 49 through 51, pages 107 and 108.

11. Make two ribbon candy roses using 6" of the ⅝" wide embroidery silk ribbon and refer to the straight ruching photos in Chapter 5, Exercise 1 on page 77.

12. Make two lavender/pink rosettes using 2¼" of ¼" wide ruffled edge ribbon for each rosette and the u-gather technique diagrams 40 through 42, page 103. Sew three seed beads in the center of each rosette.

13. Make three curved leaves using 2" of ¼" wide yellow/green ruffled edge ribbon for each leaf and the curved leaf technique diagrams 123 through 126, pages 155 and 156.

14. Make two "Figure 8 Loop" leaves using 3" of ⅛" wide medium green silk-satin ribbon for each "leaf" and diagrams 29 and 30 on page 83.

15. Referring to the detail photo of the flower composition, stitch the flowers, stamens, and leaves to the crinoline. Cut away the excess crinoline. Stitch or glue the flower composition to the side, or the top of the pincushion.

Optional embellishing: *Add some sterling silver sewing tools, a fancy bead stickpin, or an old brooch.*

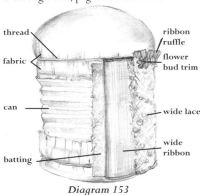

Diagram 153

Wedding Bouquet

Bias-cut silk roses and wide milliners grosgrain present the perfect elements for a bouquet for any occasion, and especially for a bridal bouquet. The bouquet shown on page 203 has a large tea rose surrounded by six smaller folded roses. The leaves are knotted loops of ribbon.

You will need:

36" pink grosgrain or heavy silk ribbon or fabric, 3" wide

12" pink/cream bias-cut silk ribbon, 1½" wide

1½ yd. pink/cream bias-cut silk ribbon, 1½" wide

1½ yd. pale pink bias-cut silk ribbon, 1½" wide

56" pink/cream bias-cut silk ribbon, 2½" wide

2½ yd. apple green bias-cut silk ribbon, 1" wide

1 yd. olive green bias-cut silk ribbon, 1" wide

1 yd. creamy peach bias satin cording, ¼" wide

7 (9") pieces of wire, 20-gauge

20 pearls

Steps:

1. Referring to pleating diagram 33, page 86, make the large pleated ruffle using 36" of wide pink grosgrain ribbon. Divide and pin the ribbon into sixteen pleats. Each pleat is 1" and overlaps by ½". Stitch the pleats at one edge with two rows of stitching. Sew the two raw edges together so the pleated ribbon forms a circle of pleated ribbon. A slight gathering of the inside edge of the pleated ribbon may be needed to keep it all flat. Set aside.

> **Tip:** *If the pleated ruffle sags, brace it with a fabric-covered circle on the underside of the ruffle. Make a hole in the cardboard circle for the stems to go through, and cover the circle with fabric. Glue this to the underside of the ruffle.*

2. Make a stemmed tea rose. This version of the tea rose has a coil center and two sizes of rolled corner outer petals. All the ribbons are pink/cream bias-cut silk ribbon. Use 12" of 1½" wide pink/cream ribbon for the coiled rose center and refer to the upright coil u-gather diagrams 49 through 51, pages 107 and 108. **Note:** Before stitching the coiled center of the rose, insert a 9" piece of 20-gauge wire into the center and secure with a little white glue. Use 12" of 2½" wide pink/cream ribbon for three rolled corner petals (each petal uses 4" of ribbon) and refer to diagrams 100 through 107 on pages 138 and 139. Use 44" of 2½" wide silk ribbon for eight rolled corner petals (each petal uses 5½" of ribbon) and the rolled corner petal diagrams 100 through 107 on pages 138 and 139. To assemble the rose, stitch the three smaller petals to the coiled rose center first. Overlap, and stitch the eight larger petals around the smaller petals in a clockwise direction. Complete the rose by cutting away the excess ribbon from the base of the rose. Cover the raw edges at the base of the completed rose, with 4" of apple green bias-cut silk ribbon wrapped as you would floral tape.

3. Make six folded roses using 18" of 1½" wide bias-cut silk ribbon for each rose and the folded rose technique, diagram 87 through 92, pages 132 and 133. Make three of the roses from the pale pink bias-cut ribbon and three roses from the pink/cream ribbon. When you begin to make this rose, insert a 9" piece of 20-gauge stem wire into the center of the rose, then complete the folding and rolling of the ribbon until all the ribbon is used up. When the rose is completed, cover the raw edges at the base of the rose with 3" of apple green bias-cut silk ribbon.

4. Make six knotted loop "leaves" using 6" of 1" wide apple green bias-cut ribbon and the knot petal technique diagram 16, page 71. Sew or glue one loop leaf between each of the smaller roses, when you are composing the bouquet.

5. Make seven stem covers using two different green ribbons. Make four stem covers each using 8" of 1" wide olive green ribbon, and make three stem covers using 8" of 1" wide apple green ribbon and the stem cover technique diagram 11, page 64.

Putting the Bouquet Together:

Gather all the stemmed roses in your hand with the smaller folded roses surrounding the large tea rose at the center. Insert the roses into the hole at the center of the ruffle. Gather/sew the ruffled ribbon to tightly fit around the roses. Wrap the creamy peach cording around the base of the roses under the ruffle and down about 3". Secure with stitches or glue. Tie a bow using 18" of the creamy peach cording around the stems.

Optional embellishing idea: *Randomly sew small pearls to several of the flower petals and the pink ruffle.*

RIGHT: A bouquet of creamy pink silk ribbon roses sits amongst wedding day remembrances and a half doll lampshade.

Rosebud and Rosette Boutonniere

Rosebuds are the perfect choice for a boutonnière-sized arrangement. Combine the roses with some rosettes and a few leaves and you have the makings of something very pretty. The flowers can be tied together with a bow or inserted into a sweet silver lapel pin. (Remember Agatha Christie's famous Belgian detective, Hercule Poirot? He always wore a lapel vase pin with a flower in it!)

You will need:

7½" pink wire-edge ribbon, 1" wide

14½" pink/green wire-edge ribbon, 1" wide

21½" pink/plum wire-edge ribbon, 1" wide

10½" cream double-faced satin silk, ⅜" wide

10½" olive green ombre wire-edge ribbon, 1½" wide

54" apple green bias-cut silk ribbon, ⅝" wide

3 double-headed yellow stamens

9 (4") pieces of wire, 32-gauge

Steps:

1. Make three rosebuds. The roses are made in two parts—an upright coil rose center (refer to diagrams 49 through 51, pages 107 and 108) and three surrounding rolled corner petals (refer to diagrams 100 through 107, pages 138 through 140). The center of one rose uses 7" of pink/plum ribbon and the outer petals use 2½" of pink/plum per petal. The second rose center uses 7" of pink/plum ribbon and the outer petals use 2½" of pink ribbon per petal. The third rose center uses 7" of pink/green ribbon and the outer petals use 2½" of pink/green ribbon per petal. Before stitching the coil rose centers, sew or glue a 4" wire into the folded start of the coil rose. Evenly arrange and sew the petals to the rose center so the petals are slightly taller than the coil center. Finish the stems with 6" of green bias-cut silk ribbon, as you would use floral tape.

2. Make three cream rosettes using 3½" of cream silk-satin ribbon for each rosette, referring to the u-gather technique, diagrams 40 through 42, page 103. Use one doubled-over yellow stamen per rosette center. Glue a 4" piece of wire to each stamen stem. Insert the stemmed stamens into the rosette before the rosette gathering is tightly secured. Cover the raw edges of the rosette and stem with 6" of green bias-cut silk ribbon.

3. Make three prairie point leaves using 3½" of olive ombre ribbon for each leaf and the prairie point technique, diagrams 118 through 121, page 153. Insert a 4" wire into the stitch line before gathering tightly. Finish the raw edges and the stem with 6" of green bias-cut silk ribbon.

 Tip: *Make the leaves slightly smaller by stitching the gathering line up ¼" from the base edge.*

4. Arrange the posy in your hand and tie the stems with a piece of ribbon, or insert the stems into a silver lapel vase pin.

Chapter 12

More Challenging Projects

*This chapter contains projects that will
test your skills in flower
construction and
design. Within each
project, you will be
guided, step-by-step,
through each of the
flowers and elements,
with references
back to the
techniques
should you
forget how a leaf or
flower is made. There
are many beautiful
projects that you'll be
tempted to make—go
ahead and try them!*

This small brooch, made in the vintage style of the 1920s, features the flat rose, blossoms, and dangling buds. If you can manage to create a vintage flat rose that looks like any of the flat roses in this book, then you will have mastered this rose!

You will need:

5" pale green jacquard ribbon, fringed

28" pale pink single- (or double-) faced silk-satin ribbon, ⅝" wide

9" pink/peach ombre ribbon, ⅜" wide

3" sage green double-faced silk-satin ribbon, ⅜" wide

6¾" pale green gold edge ruffled ribbon, ¼" wide

9" pale green gimp or fancy thread

10 green stamens

4 gold stamens

5 pink stamen buds

20 crystal seed beads

2" x 5" piece of crinoline

2" x 3" piece of felt or ultrasuede

Pin back

Vintage Brooch with Buds

Steps:

1. Cut a 1¼" strip from the edge of the crinoline piece, and set it aside for the flat rose construction.

2. Turn under ⅛", the raw edges of the fringed jacquard ribbon. Stitch very small running stitches along the bottom edge of the ribbon so it gathers into a half-circle arch. Position this near the top center of the crinoline (the fringing will barely hang over the top edge of the crinoline). With very small stitches, sew the bottom edge of the ribbon in an arch, and sew down the top edge every ¼", adding crystal seed beads as you go. Set aside until the flowers are made.

3. Make one vintage flat rose using 22" of the ⅝" wide pink single-faced silk-satin ribbon and the flat rose technique diagrams 82 through 86, pages 129 and 130. Start this rose by tacking the knot to the center of a 1¼" circle of crinoline. Fold the ribbon until it is all used. Try to keep just the *folds* in the ribbon showing, but don't despair if the woven edge of the ribbon sometimes shows.

4. Make three vintage flat buds using the ⅝" wide pink single-faced satin ribbon and the basic bud technique, diagrams 76 through 79, page 125. Each bud uses 2" of ribbon and 3" of gimp for each stem. Use 1" of ⅜" wide sage green satin to cover the raw edges on the buds. Center the green ribbon over the raw end of the stemmed bud, and fold it around to the back. Tack where the ribbon overlaps in the back. With very neat, tiny stitches sew the top edge of the calyx to the bud and gather the bottom edge around the stem.

5. Make two blossoms using the pink/peach ombre ribbon and the four-petal u-gather stitch pattern, diagrams 70 through 71 page 119. Each blossom uses 4½" of ribbon, and a mix of two green/yellow stamens and five gold stamens for the center. Prepare the stamens as in diagrams 3 and 4, page 56.

6. Make three curved leaves using 2¼" of pale green, gold-edge ribbon per leaf and the curved leaf technique diagrams 123 through 126, pages 155 and 156.

7. To complete the composition, sew the unbent pink stamen buds at a slight angle over the arched fringed jacquard ribbon. Sew on the remaining elements as shown in the photo, except for the large flat rose. Sew the large flat vintage rose over the other elements, being sure that the bottom of the arched ribbon is covered and the blossoms sit at the side of the rose.

8. Cut away the excess crinoline. Sew a pin back to the felt or ultrasuede backing and glue that to the back of the crinoline. Trim away the excess backing.

Small ribbon flowers are the perfect elements to add to a pendant. In fact, they can make up the whole pendant! While not a difficult project, the scale of the ribbons makes these two pendant designs somewhat fiddly.

For a Wild "Hairy" Pendant, you will need:

60" of any ¼" wide ribbon, in any color combination

1 yd. eyelash threads in any color

1 yd. variegated yarn in any color

2 yd. hand-dyed rattail

2¼" circle of matteboard

2¼" circle of thin batting or felt

3" circle of beige dupioni silk fabric

2¼" circle of ultra suede or felt

25 iridescent pebble beads

Fancy button, ¾" to 1" wide

White glue

Two Pendants

Steps:

1. Make ten loop "flowers" using an assortment of ¼" wide ribbons and the loop technique, diagrams 27 and 28, page 82. Each flower uses about 6" of ¼" wide ribbon and has five to six loops. Set the flowers aside when made.

2. Lightly glue the batting to the cardboard circle. Cover the circle with fabric by stitching around the fabric and pulling the gathering tightly over the batting/cardboard. Refer to diagram 148, page 178.

3. Glue the button to the center front of the fabric-covered circle. If the button has a shank, pierce the shank through the cardboard and anchor on the back with a piece of wire.

4. Using 2" of rattail, make a loop and glue it to the top of the back of the pendant. This is for the neck cord to go through.

5. Arrange three to four layers of the yarn and eyelash thread around the edge of the circle. Stitch the eyelash/yarns to the fabric in several places to secure. Embellish with beads if desired.

6. Arrange and glue the loop flowers around the button, until the entire surface of the pendant is full.

7. Make a beaded tassel using 9" of the rattail cording. Cut it into three pieces and thread pebble beads onto the rattail and knot in place. Glue the rattail pieces to the bottom and back of the pendant.

8. Cover the back of the pendant with ultrasuede, leather, fabric, or felt.

9. Using pebble beads in random placement, thread them onto the rattail neck cord. Knot them in place with simple overhand knots. Tie a simple knot for the neck cord closure or use jewelry findings.

Steps:

1. Make twelve folded roses. Each rose uses 5½" of ⁷⁄₁₆" wide bias-cut silk ribbon and the folded rose technique, diagrams 87 through 92, pages 132 and 133.

2. Make six knot roses. Each rose uses 2¼" of ¼" bias silk-satin cord. Tie a plain knot in the cord and turn the raw ends under the knot. Review diagram 15 and the photos in Chapter 5 for knot flowers, page 70. Remove some of the white inner cording if it shows. Sew one small bead to the center of each rose.

> **Tip:** *Don't precut the cord. Simply tie the knot and then cut the cord.*

3. Lightly glue the batting to the cardboard circle.

4. Cover the circle with fabric by stitching around the edge of the fabric and pulling the gathering tightly over the batting/cardboard.

5. Glue/stitch the button to the center front of the fabric-covered circle.

6. Sew the silk-satin cord around the outer edge of the fabric-covered circle.

7. Make a small loop using 2" of the silk-satin cord and glue it to the top and back of the pendant. This is for the neck cord to go through.

8. Glue six folded roses around the button.

9. Alternate six knot roses and six folded roses and glue them around the outer area of the pendant.

10. Cover the back of the pendant with ultrasuede, leather, fabric, or felt.

11. Slip the neck cord through the loop and tie a simple knot or use jewelry findings for the closure.

12. Optional: Use an assortment of fancy beads to make a dangle/tassel at the bottom of the pendant if desired.

For a Rose Pendant, you will need:

66" earth-toned bias-cut silk ribbon, ⁷⁄₁₆" wide

2 yd. earth-toned bias-cut silk-satin cording, ⅛" wide

2" circle of matteboard

2" circle of thin batting

2¾" circle of beige dupioni silk fabric

Fancy button, ⅝" to ¾" wide

6 small garnet beads

White glue

Optional: beads for a tassel

A combination of small and medium flowers make up this brooch, which is a perfect size for a coat lapel, an album cover, or a memory book. The photo on the next page shows the brooch pinned to a vintage sewing roll made of 6" wide silk ribbon.

You will need:

9" bridal ivory bias-cut silk-satin ribbon, 2½" wide

6" bridal ivory bias-cut silk ribbon, 1½" wide

5" pink pleated georgette ribbon, ⅝" wide

8" dusty pink single-faced silk-satin ribbon, ⅝" wide

7" pale pink silk ribbon, 1½" wide

7" dark pink silk ribbon, 1½" wide

7½" white/pink ruffled-edge ribbon, ⅝" wide

7½" green gimp

9" pale green wired ribbon, 1" wide

7" lime green silk-satin ribbon, ⅜" wide

4" green pleated georgette ribbon, ⅝" wide

6" lace, 2" wide

20 gold seed beads

1", pin back, 1"

3" square of crinoline

3" square beige leather or felt

Spring Brooch - Ribbon Roses and Bell Flowers

Steps:

1. Make a lace fan by stitching along the 6" edge of the 2" wide lace. Gather tightly and set aside.

2. Make one cream silk cabochon rose. The rose is made in two parts. The three outer petals each use 3" of the 2½" wide cream bias-cut silk-satin ribbon and the top fold edge u-gather technique diagrams 55, 56, 57, and 59, pages 110 and 111. The rose center uses 6" of 1½" wide cream bias-cut silk ribbon and the top fold coil u-gather technique diagram 58, page 111. Sew this rose center firmly to the middle of a ¾" piece of crinoline. Stitch the three outer petals around the rose center, referring to diagram 59, page 111.

3. Make one pink pleated rose. The rose is made in two parts. The rose center is made with 8" of ⅝" wide silk ribbon and the upright coil u-gather technique diagrams 49 through 51, pages 107 and 108. The outer ruffle is made from 5" of ⅝" wide pink pleated ribbon and using the u-gather technique, diagram 40, page 103. Gather the pleated ribbon to fit around the rose center. Stitch both parts together with the rose being well seated into the ruffled outer petals. Trim the excess raw edges from the back.

4. Make two silk rosette roses. Each rose uses 7" of 1½" wide silk ribbon and the bottom ⅔ fold u-gather technique, diagrams 52 through 54, page 109. Sew ten seed beads to the center of each rose.

5. Make three white/pink bell flowers. Each flower uses 2½" of ⅝" wide ruffled-edge ribbon and uses the tube technique, diagrams 34 through 37, pages 95 and 96. Review the section on Bell Flowers in Chapter 6. Use 2½" of gimp for the stem.

6. Make three pale green prairie point leaves. Each leaf uses 3" of the 1" wide pale green wired ribbon and the prairie point technique, diagrams 118 through 121, page 153.

7. Make three lime green half-boat leaves. Each leaf uses 2¼" of the ³/₈" wide silk-satin ribbon and the half-boat technique diagrams 132 through 136, page 161.

8. Make two olive green half-round leaves. Each leaf uses 2" of pleated georgette ribbon. Use the half round u-gather technique, diagram 122, page 154.

9. Put the composition together by stitching the lace fan to the crinoline. Arrange and stitch on the large roses, then the large leaves, followed by smaller leaves. Stitch the bell flowers to the composition last, being sure that the ends of the stems are well hidden.

10. Cut away the excess crinoline from the back of the brooch. Sew a pin back to the felt or leather and glue this to the back of the brooch. Trim the excess leather or felt from the brooch.

> **Tip:** *For a completely different look, add a porcelain cameo or porcelain flapper head (sew-on style) to the center of the brooch composition. Very elegant!*

Jardinière with Small Pink and Cream Roses

Ten techniques are used to make this sweet vase of mixed roses, blossoms, and bells, and all of them are easily accomplished. The arrangement measures 6½" wide x 5½" tall and will fit into many of the standard ready-made frames available at the frame shop.

You will need:

9" cream single-faced satin-silk ribbon, ⅝" wide

9" cream shirred ribbon, ¾" wide

22" pink single-faced satin-silk ribbon, ⅝" wide

6" pink pleated georgette ribbon, ⅝" wide

9" pink/gray ombre wired ribbon, 1" wide

14" dusty pink silk ribbon, 1½" wide

7" dark pink silk ribbon, 1½" wide

7" pale pink silk ribbon, 1½" wide

25" white ribbon, ⅝" wide

12" pink shirred ribbon, ¾" wide

10" dark olive green gimp

18" olive green ombre wire-edged ribbon, 1" wide

18" lime green double-faced satin-silk ribbon, ⅜" wide

10" olive green pleated georgette ribbon, ⅝" wide

6" square of crinoline

18 crystal seed beads

25 gold stamens

Small jardinière, 2¾" x 1¾"

Steps:

1. Make one cream rose. The rose is made in two parts from two different ribbons. The center uses 9" of ⅝" wide cream single sided satin-silk and the folded rose with gathered extension technique diagram 93, page 134. Use 5" of the ribbon for the mini folded rose and then gather the remaining 4" of ribbon and coil it around the folded rose. For the three outer petals, use 3" of ¾" wide cream shirred ribbon per petal and the u-gather technique, diagram 40, page 103. Gather each petal tightly. Overlap and stitch the petals high up on the rose center.

2. Make one ruffled pink rose. The rose is made in two parts from two different ribbons. The center uses 9" of ⅝" wide pink single-face satin-silk and the folded rose with gathered extension technique diagram 93, page 134. Use 5" of the ribbon for the mini folded rose and then gather the remaining 4" of ribbon and coil it around the folded rose. The outer ruffle uses 6" of ⅝" wide pink pleated georgette ribbon and the u-gather technique diagram 40, page 103. Fit the ruffle around the pink rose center about half way up the height of the rose, tighten the ruffle, and secure with stitches.

3. Make two small pink folded roses using 8" and 5" of ⅝" wide pink single-faced satin-silk and the folded rose technique, diagrams 87 through 92, pages 132 and 133.

4. Make one pink/gray folded rose using 9" of 1" wide pink/gray ombre wired ribbon and the folded rose technique, diagrams 87 through 92, pages 132 and 133.

5. Make four large double rosette roses. Each rose uses 7" of 1½" wide silk ribbon and the fold-up ⅔ u-gather technique, diagrams 52 through 54, page 109. The rosettes will show two layers of ribbon when completed. Make two of the roses dusty pink, one rose pale pink, and one rose dark pink. Stitch nine seed beads in the center of one dusty pink rose and the dark pink rose. For the two remaining roses—one dusty pink and one pale pink—dip the entire rose in a glass of water and quickly remove it. Pat dry to take out most of the water and then scrunch the rose in your fingertips. Fluff out the inner petals and leave to dry on a paper towel. When dry, the petals will have a lovely old-rose look about them.

6. Make five white blossoms using 5" of ⅝" wide white ribbon per flower and the four-petal continuous u-gather technique, diagrams 70 and 71, page 109. Gather the ribbon tightly and insert five stamens into the center before securing the petals together. Do not cut the stems as they will be tucked under the other flowers and leaves.

7. Make four pink bells using 3" of ¾" wide pink shirred ribbon for each bell, and 2½" of dark olive green gimp for each stem, referring to the bell flower tube technique, diagrams 34 through 37, pages 95 and 96 and Bell Flowers on page 97.

8. Make six prairie point leaves using 3" of 1" wide olive green ombre wire-edge ribbon and the prairie point technique, diagrams 118 through 121, page 153.

9. Make seven half-boat leaves using 2½" of ⅜" wide lime green double-faced satin-silk ribbon and the half-boat leaf technique, diagrams 132 through 136, page 161.

10. Make five half-round leaves using 2" of ⅝" wide olive green pleated georgette ribbon per leaf and the half-round leaf technique, diagram 122, page 154.

Putting the Composition Together

Sew the flowers to the crinoline in the following order:

1. Cream petal rose, pink pleated rose, and two scrunched silk rosette/roses.

2. Two silk rosette/roses, one wired folded pink rose, two pink silk folded roses.

3. Add assorted leaves around the roses.

4. Add five blossoms and four bells.

5. Glue the jardinière to the crinoline, under the flowers. Trim away the excess crinoline.

There are twenty-one flowers and twelve leaves in this spectacular floral composition. The flowers are sewn to a long piece of hand-dyed appliqué lace, and it is suitable for use on a hat, a boudoir pillow, or a lingerie bag, or . . . you'll think of many beautiful uses for these flowers.

You will need:

27" gold satin-silk ribbon, ⅜" wide

12" cream shirred ribbon, ½" wide

15¾" cream satin-silk ribbon, ⅝" wide

24" wine shirred ribbon, ½" wide

11" plum ombre wire-edge ribbon, 1" wide

9" burgundy gold-edged ribbon, ¼" wide

5" wine pleated georgette ribbon, 1" wide

15" pink/lavender ruffled-edge ribbon, ¼" wide

8" green ruffled-edge ribbon, ¼" wide

8" green ruffled-gold edge ribbon, ¼" wide

8" yellow/green ruffled-edge ribbon, ¼" wide

Hand-dyed lace appliqué, 10" x 3"

9 burgundy seed beads

6 crystal seed beads

6 wine stamens

2" square of crinoline

Small Flowers on Lace

Steps:

1. Make two large gold roses. The rose is made in two parts using two different ribbons and two techniques. The folded-rose center uses 4½" of ⅜" wide gold satin-silk ribbon per rose and the folded rose technique, diagrams 87 through 92, pages 132 and 133. The outer ruffle uses 6" of ½" wide cream shirred ribbon per rose and the u-gather technique, diagram 40, page 103. Encircle each of the 4½" gold folded roses with the ruffle and secure. The rose center should be deeply seated into the ruffle.

2. Make three cream cabochon roses. The rose is made in two parts using two colors of ribbon and two techniques. The folded rose center uses 4" of ⅜" wide gold satin-silk ribbon per rose and the folded rose technique, diagrams 87 through 92, pages 132 and 133. The three outer petals use 1¾" per petal of ⅝" wide cream satin-silk ribbon each and are made using the u-gather technique, diagram 40 page 103. Overlap and sew the three petals together so they form a very cupped circle, into which a gold folded rose is deeply seated and secured. Trim the excess ribbon from the back of the rose.

3. Make two small gold folded roses using 3" of ⅜" wide gold satin-silk ribbon per rose and the folded rose technique, diagrams 87 through 92, pages 132 and 133.

4. Make three medium wine folded roses using 5" of ½" wide wine shirred ribbon and the folded rose technique, diagrams 87 through 92, pages 132 and 133.

5. Make one large pink/plum rosette rose. The rose is made in two parts using two colors of ribbon and two techniques. The mini folded rose center uses 3" of ½" wide wine shirred ribbon and the folded-rose technique, diagrams 87 through 92, pages 132 and 133. The outer double ruffle uses 5" of 1" wide plum ombre wire-edge ribbon and the ⅔ fold u-gather technique, diagrams 52 through 54, page 109. Leave a small hole at the center of the rosette so the folded rose can be fitted into the center snuggly.

6. Make one large burgundy coil rose. The rose is made in two parts using two colors of ribbon and two techniques. The upright coil center uses 4½" of ¼" wide burgundy gold-edged ribbon and the upright coil u-gather technique, diagrams 49 through 51, pages 107 and 108. The outer ruffle uses 6" of ½" wide wine shirred ribbon and the u-gather technique, diagram 40, page 103. Stitch the upright coil rose to the top of the wine ruffle.

7. Make one small burgundy upright coil rose using 4½" of ¼" wide burgundy gold-edged ribbon and the upright coil u-gather technique, diagrams 49 through 51, pages 107 and 108.

8. Make two fuchsias using 3" of 1" wide plum ombre wire-edge ribbon per flower and the fuchsia technique, diagrams 80 and 81, page 127. Each flower uses three wine stamens.

9. Make one plum rose using 5" of 1" wide wine pleated georgette ribbon and the upright coil u-gather technique, diagrams 49 through 51, pages 107 and 108.

10. Make two pink/lavender spiral rosettes using 4"of ¼" wide pink/lavender ruffled-edge ribbon and the u-gather technique, diagrams 40, 47, and 48, pages 103 and 105. Use a ¾" circle of crinoline and sew the end of the gathering to the center of the crinoline. Spiral the gathered ribbon around two times and secure with stitches as you go. Sew three crystal seed beads at the center of each rosette. Cut away the excess crinoline. The flower will be flat.

11. Make three pink/lavender rosettes using 2¼" of ¼" wide pink/lavender ruffled-edge ribbon and the u-gather technique diagrams 40 through 42, page 103. Use three burgundy seed beads at the center of each rosette.

12. Make twelve curved leaves using 2" of ¼" wide ruffled-edge ribbon for each leaf and the curved leaf technique, diagrams 123 through 126, pages 155 and 156. Make four green leaves, four gold edge leaves, and four yellow/green leaves.

Putting The Composition Together

Use the photo as a guide for stitching on the flowers and leaves. Start with the large flowers and gradually add the flowers in descending order of size. Tuck in the leaves under and around the flowers.

A "Ribbon Board" is handy to have when you are needing a laptop surface for your ribbonwork. An antique set of sterling silver ribbon bodkins is at the top of the board, while reproduction sterling silver tools are scattered around the board.

This project is so useful for your ribbonwork. The board acts like a large, flat pincushion—a working surface for pinning completed flowers to. It's also a surface upon which to design the ribbon flowers into a composition.

You will need:

10" x 14" piece of foam core board, ½" thick

10" x 14" piece of matteboard

2 (14" x 18") pieces of matching fabric (silk, cotton, lightweight jacquard)

3 (10" x 14") pieces of batting, ¼" thick

50" olive green chenille-edge ribbon, ½" wide

9" gold chenille-edge ribbon, ½" wide

12" autumn-tone flower bud trim

6" burgundy double-faced satin-silk ribbon, ⅜" wide

8" burgundy chenille-edge ribbon, ½" wide

6" pale gold double-faced satin-silk ribbon, ⅜" wide

8" gold pleated georgette ribbon, ⅝" wide

6" gold/bronze ombre ribbon, ⅜" wide

8" gold chenille-edge ribbon, ½" wide

18" pink gold-edge ribbon, ¼" wide

12" olive velvet ribbon, ¾" wide

10½" sheer olive pleated ribbon, ⅝" wide

10" yellow/green ruffled-edge ribbon, ¼" wide

5" square of crinoline

16 gold seed beads

White glue

Optional: 3" x 5" piece of heavy weight hand-dyed lace appliqué

Ribbon Board with Fancy Flowers

Making this board is very easy, and decorating it is a lot of fun. Make it as simple or as complicated as you like. When selecting a fabric to cover the board, keep the pattern simple. If the flower composition shown in the photo is a little intimidating, perhaps a simpler, large flower like the coil rose (see the Hat project, page 189) would be a lovely substitution for the composition shown.

The instructions for the ribbon board decorations will give colors as shown, but please feel free to make this project in colors and ribbons of your choice.

Steps:

1. Cover the foam core board. Lightly brush on glue to the foam core and adhere the three layers of batting. Place one piece of fabric over the batting and glue the edges on the back of the board. Miter the corners, referring to diagram 147, page 177.

2. Decorate the bottom left corner of the covered foam core board with a ribbon strap. Use 9" of gold chenille-edge ribbon and 9" of flower bud trim. Place the trim on the ribbon and sew them together using a seed bead on every flowerhead. Place this embellished ribbon in the bottom left corner, gluing the overage to the back of the covered board. This becomes a "strap" that papers or scissors could be inserted under.

3. Cover the matteboard with fabric and then glue the matteboard to the back of the covered foam core. Use clothespins, or a heavy book, to hold the boards together until the glue dries. When dry, glue the green chenille-edge ribbon over the joined edge.

4. Make three large roses. The roses are made in two parts. The center is either a folded rose or a folded rose with gathered extension, while the outer petals are one large ruffle. Make one burgundy rose using 6" of burgundy satin-silk ribbon for the folded rose with gathered extension center, diagram 93, page 134 and 8" of burgundy chenille-edge ribbon for the outer u-gather ruffle, diagram 40, page 103. Make one pale gold rose using 6" of pale gold satin-silk for the folded rose with gathered extension center, diagram 93, page 134 and 8" of gold sheer pleated ribbon for the u-gather ruffle, diagram 40, page 103. Make one dark gold rose using 6" of bronze/gold ombre ribbon for a folded rose center, diagrams 87 through 92, pages 132 and 133, and 8" of gold chenille-edge ribbon for the outer u-gather ruffle, diagram 40, page 103.

5. Make four upright coil roses. Each rose uses 4½" of pink gold-edge ribbon and the upright coil technique, diagrams 49 through 51, pages 107 and 108.

6. Make eleven curved leaves using the three different green ribbons and the curved leaf technique, diagrams 123 through 126, pages 155 and 156. Make three leaves using 4" of velvet ribbon per leaf. Make three leaves using 3½" of olive pleated georgette ribbon per leaf. Make five leaves using 2" of the narrow yellow/green ruffled-edge ribbon per leaf.

Putting the Composition Together

When all the flowers and leaves are made, arrange the flower composition on a piece of crinoline. If using a piece of lace cut up some of the parts and sew one or two pieces to the crinoline as a base upon which to set ribbon flowers and leaves. Sew the three main roses to the center of the crinoline in a triangle shape. Add the velvet and pleated large leaves, followed by the small pink coil roses. Add any other small lace pieces. Add three small leaves and the remaining piece of flower bud trim. Trim away the excess crinoline and pin or stitch the composition to the top left of the board.

Sew one pink coil rose and two small leaves to the center of the gold chenille "strap" holder, bottom left.

The flowers on this lace pillow are all made with bias-cut silk ribbons of various widths. The roses are made with the satin bias-cut silk and the other flowers are made from the plain bias-cut silk. The prairie point leaves are made from wire-edge ribbon.

Bias-Cut Silk Flowers on a Pillow

You will need:

36" pink bias-cut silk-satin ribbon, 2½" wide

15" creamy pink bias-cut silk ribbon, 1" wide

24" creamy pink bias-cut silk ribbon, 1½" wide

6" cream bias-cut silk-satin ribbon, 1½" wide

9" cream bias-cut silk-satin ribbon, 2½" wide

6" peachy/pink bias-cut silk-satin ribbon, 1½" wide

9" peachy/pink bias-cut silk-satin ribbon, 2½" wide

16¼" peachy/pink bias-cut silk-satin ribbon, 2½" wide

10½" blue bias-cut silk ribbon, 1½" wide

6" purple bias-cut silk ribbon, ⅝" wide

10½" olive green ombre wire-edge ribbon, 1½" wide

7" hunter green ombre wire-edge ribbon, 1½" wide

3½" lavender/green ombre wire-edge ribbon, 1½" wide

7 yellow stamens

3 yellow seed beads

2" square of crinoline

6" x 5" rectangle of crinoline

Steps:

1. Make one large pink coil rose using 36" of 2½" wide pink bias-cut silk-satin ribbon and the top fold upright coil u-gather technique, diagrams 55 and 58, pages 110 and 111. Gather the ribbon to about 10" in length. Do not secure the gathering yet. Thread a second needle. Coil the gathered ribbon around the center, taking a few stitches as you go to secure all the layers. Once the ribbon is coiled, stitch through all the layers at the base of the rose to secure. Trim excess ribbon at the base.

2. Make one large creamy pink peony. This flower is made in two parts using two different widths of ribbon but using the same frayed and snipped straight gather technique, diagrams 24 and 25, pages 80 and 81. Use 15" of 1" wide creamy pink bias-cut silk ribbon and coil the ribbon as you would for a rose. For the outer ruffles, use 24" of 1½" wide creamy pink bias-cut silk ribbon. Gather the ribbon tightly and coil it around the smaller frayed center about one and one-half times.

3. Make one basic cream cabochon rose. The rose is made in two parts, and the ribbons are folded to measure half of their original width. The coil rose center uses 6" of 1½" wide cream bias-cut silk-satin ribbon and the top fold upright coil u-gather technique, diagrams 55, 58, and 59, pages 110 and 111. Gather the ribbon and coil it into a rose shape. Cut off the raw edges. Stitch this to the center of a ¾" circle of crinoline. The three outer petals use 3" of 2½" wide cream bias-cut silk-satin ribbon per petal and the top fold u-gather technique, diagrams 55 through 57, pages 110 and 111. Stitch the first petal over the coil rose center and under the crinoline. Overlap the second petal and stitch it over the rose center. Stitch the third petal over the rose center—the rose is now enclosed. Refer to diagram 59, page 111. **Note:** Attaching the second and third petals requires patience.

   4. Make one large peachy/pink cabochon rose. It's constructed the same way as the basic cream cabochon rose, but with the addition of five more outer u-gather petals. The coil rose center uses 6" of 1½" wide peachy/pink bias-cut silk-satin ribbon. The three middle petals use 3" of 2½" wide peachy/pink bias-cut silk-satin ribbon per petal. The five outer petals use 3¼" of 2½" wide peachy/pink bias-cut silk-satin ribbon and the top fold u-gather technique, diagrams 55 through 57, pages 110 and 111. On a 1" circle of crinoline, evenly arrange the five outer petals around the edge. There will be a ⅝" area of crinoline showing at the center and this is where you will stitch the basic peachy/pink cabochon rose center made earlier.

> **Tip:** *To encourage the cabochon rosebud petals to "sit down" after the rosebud is attached to the crinoline with the outer petals, take a few hidden stitches under each of the three petals.*

   5. Make one mini hydrangea using 10½" of 1½" wide blue bias-cut silk ribbon and the cut flower instructional Exercise 2 in Chapter 6, page 92. Make seven individual florets using 1½" square of ribbon for each. Place one yellow stamen in each center. Wrap the stems with 2" of floral tape. Combine all stems and glue to a 3" piece of 22-gauge wire and wrap with floral tape.

   6. Make one purple rosette using 7" of ⅝" wide purple bias-cut silk ribbon and the u-gather technique, diagrams 40 through 42, page 103. Use three yellow seed beads at the center.

   7. Make six prairie point leaves using 3½" per leaf of 1½" wide assorted green wire-edge ribbons and the prairie point leaf technique, diagrams 118 through 121, page 153. Make three leaves using olive green ombre ribbon; make two leaves using hunter green ombre ribbon; and make one using lavender/green ombre ribbon.

Putting The Composition Together

   Using the photo at right as a guide, sew the main flowers to the crinoline followed by the smaller flowers and leaves. Everything should overlap. Use the flowers on a cushion, or in any manner that you would like—on an album, as a wall hanging or under glass in a frame.

Bias-cut silk ribbons make up into many beautiful flowers as shown on this lace pillow. The antique pillow sham with ribbonwork is French, circa 1915.

Vanity boxes were a commonly used item on the dressing table of most women during the 1920s. This box, although new, looks old because of the subtle color scheme and the use of vintage gold braids.

You will need:

3" x 5" fabric print

2 (5" x 3") pieces of thin cotton padding, ¼" thick

16" green loop trim

26" burgundy/green suede ribbon, ⅝" wide

24" gold/pink wire-edge ribbon, 1" wide

12" mauve wire-edge ribbon, 1" wide

6" plum pleated georgette ribbon, ⅝" wide

11" blue ribbon, ½" wide

4½" yellow gold-edge ribbon, ⅜" wide

9" pale gold double-faced satin-silk ribbon, ⅜" wide

14" purple/red ruffled-edge ribbon, ¼" wide

6" soft green velvet ribbon, ¾" wide

10" moss green wire-edge ribbon, 1" wide

7½" red/green wire-edge ribbon, 1" wide

10" yellow/green ruffled-edge ribbon, ¼" wide

6 gold stamens

40 mauve seed beads

6 gold seed beads

5 faceted metallic beads, 4mm

3 (1" diameter) circles of crinoline

Optional: 35" vintage or new, gold braid, ⅝" wide (for framing the composition)

Vintage Style Ribbon Flowers For a Box Top

The focus of this project is the lid design which features a fabric print and vintage-style ribbon flowers. While the photo shows the ribbonwork atop a box (which was made from a box kit), you might use the design for something else. Whether you choose to put the design on a papier mâché box, in a picture frame, on a pillow, as a wall hanging, or on a hat box, you'll have a beautiful heirloom to hand down to the next generation. Feel free to change the ribbon colors (not the ribbon widths) for ones that you may have in your ribbon stash. The finished design is 7" by 9".

Steps:

These instructions reflect the ribbonwork being sewn directly to the fabric and not crinoline. If you are using a lightweight fabric, you will want to stabilize the back of the fabric with a lightweight woven or fusible interfacing.

1. Cut two pieces of thin padding ⅛" smaller than the image area of the fabric print. Layer the padding under the fabric print, then sew the print to the center of the fabric, over the gold net or lace if you are using such. Sew the green loop leaf trim around the fabric print. Add mauve seed beads, as desired, to the areas that will show.

2. Twist and pin the burgundy/green suede ribbon around the fabric print and tack it in hidden places to secure. Add mauve seed beads only to the areas that will show. This step can done after the flower compositions have been stitched to the fabric, if you prefer.

3. Make three vintage flat roses. Use the flat rose technique, diagrams 82 through 86, pages 129 and 130. Make two roses using 12" of gold/pink wire-edge ribbon per rose and a 1" circle of crinoline. Make one rose using 12" of mauve wire-edge ribbon per rose and a 1" circle of crinoline.

4. Make one plum rosette using 6" of plum pleated ribbon and the u-gather technique, diagrams 40 through 42, page 103. Use three large metallic beads at the center.

5. Make one blue blossom using 6" of blue ribbon and 4-petal u-gather technique, diagrams 70 and 71, page 119. Use six gold stamens at the center.

6. Make two blue double rosettes using 2½" of blue ribbon per rosette and the bottom ⅔ fold u-gather technique, diagrams 52 through 54, page 109. Add a metallic bead to the center.

7. Make one yellow coil rose using 4½" of gold-edge ribbon and the upright u-gather technique, diagrams 49 through 51, pages 107 and 108.

8. Make two pale gold folded roses using 4½" of pale gold double-faced satin-silk ribbon for each rose and the folded rose technique, diagrams 87 through 92, pages 132 and 133.

9. Make six purple/red rosettes using 2¼" of purple/red ruffled-edge ribbon and the u-gather technique, diagrams 40 through 42, page 103. Use one gold seed bead at the center of each rosette.

10. Make ten prairie point leaves using three different ribbons and the prairie point leaf technique, diagrams 118 through 121, page 153. Make three leaves using 2" of soft green velvet ribbon per leaf; make four leaves using 2½" of moss green wire-edge ribbon per leaf; and make three leaves using 2½" of red/green wire-edge ribbon per leaf.

11. Make five curved leaves using 2" of yellow/green ruffled-edge ribbon per leaf and the curved leaf technique, diagrams 123 through 126, pages 155 and 156.

Putting the Composition Together:

Using the photo as a guide, sew the flowers and leaves to the fabric.

On the bottom right corner, sew on the two main ribbon roses (mauve and gold/pink rose), the pleated plum rosette, the large blue blossom, three velvet leaves, three moss green prairie leaves, and one red/green leaf. Add one blue double rosette, three purple/red rosettes, one pale gold folded rose, one yellow coil rose, and three yellow/green curved leaves.

In the top left corner, sew on the gold/pink rose, two red/green prairie point leaves, one moss green prairie point leaf, and two yellow/green curved leaves. Add one pale gold folded rose, one blue double rosette, and three purple/red rosettes.

These two "projects" are a lesson in design as well as flower-making techniques. Both of the designs use cabochon roses, folded roses, and rosettes, but the flowers look very different because of the differing ribbon styles used and the design layout.

Design A:
You will need:

8" plum velvet ribbon, ⅝" wide

20" mauve double ruffled-edge ribbon, ¾" wide

8" plum pleated georgette ribbon, ⅝" wide

10½" taupe pleated georgette ribbon, ⅝" wide

6¾" pink gold-edge ribbon, ¼" wide

9" green embroidery silk ribbon, ⅛" wide

12" olive green ombre wire-edge ribbon, 1" wide

9" brown ombre wire-edge ribbon, 1" wide

9" blue/brown ombre wire-edge ribbon, 1" wide

11¼" pale green ruffled edge ribbon, ¼" wide

9" flower bud trim

3 green leaf beads

9 gold seed beads

5" x 4" piece of crinoline

Two Design "Projects"

Design A: C-shape Design: Small Cabochon Roses with Mixed Flowers

This design is based on a C-shape and is used as an edge design. The design area is 4½" by 3½". It could be used on a base that has a curved or round edge, or go into the corner of a base that is square or rectangle.

The composition features two small cabochon roses with ruffled outer petals, a folded rose, rosettes, prairie point leaves, and curved leaves.

Steps:

1. Make two ruffled-edge cabochon roses. This rose is made in three parts and with three different ribbons. The knot center uses 4" of plum velvet ribbon; refer to the "knots as flowers" discussion in Chapter 5, diagram 15, page 70 for each rose. The three mauve inner petals use 2¼" per petal of mauve double ruffled-edge ribbon and the u-gather technique, diagrams 40 and 43, pages 103 and 104 for each rose. Both roses have an outer ruffle that uses the u-gather technique, diagram 40, page 103. One rose uses 8" of plum pleated georgette ribbon and the other rose uses 8" of taupe pleated georgette ribbon. Each rose is constructed the same way. Overlap and sew the three mauve inner petals together into a circle shape—it will be quite cupped. Sew the knot rose into the center of this circle of petals. Sew the ruffled ribbon under the three inner petals.

2. Make one mauve folded rose using 6" of mauve double ruffle ribbon and the folded rose technique, diagrams 87 through 92, pages 132 and 133.

3. Make one taupe pleated bud using 2½" of taupe pleated georgette ribbon and the u-gather technique, diagrams 49 through 51, pages 107 and 108. Tighten the gathering and roll the ribbon on itself so it forms a bud shape.

4. Make three pink rosettes using 2¼" of pink gold-edge ribbon and the u-gather technique, diagrams 40 through 42, page 103. Use three gold seed beads per center.

5. Make three figure 8 loop leaves using 3" of green embroidery ribbon and the Figure 8 loop technique, diagrams 29 and 30, page 83.

6. Make 10 prairie point leaves using 3" of wired ribbon in three colors (make four olive green, three blue/brown, three brown); refer to the prairie point leaf technique, diagrams 118 through 121, page 153.

7. Make five green ruffled-edge curved leaves using 2¼" of pale green ruffled ribbon and the curved leaf technique, diagrams 123 through 126, pages 155 and 156.

Putting the Composition Together:

Refer to the photo for placement of the flowers and leaves. Remember to hide all the raw edges by overlapping the leaves and flowers. The directions below reflect the flowers being stitched to crinoline. If you choose to sew the flowers directly to a piece of fabric, it's a good idea to stabilize the fabric with either a fusible or woven interfacing.

Stitch the three main roses to the crinoline. Tuck in the large leaves and then stitch on the smaller leaves and rosettes. Sew on the small taupe bud. The icing on the cake is the addition of three leaf beads and the small flower bud trim. Cut the flower bud trim into three segments and tack it in three areas of the composition, in and around the flowers and leaves. Cut away the excess crinoline and attach to the project of your choice.

Design B: Circle/Square Design: Large Cabochon Rose with Mixed Flowers

The design of this composition is very symmetrical and would typically be used in the center of a project. The design size is 4¼" x 4¼". It's based on two offset squares (one larger than the other) and a circle. It could be used on a base that is square, rectangular, or circular. The composition features a large cabochon rose, folded roses, blossoms, stamen buds, and leaves.

Design B:
You will need:

7" dusty pink wire-edge ombre ribbon, ⅝" wide

7½" pale pink grosgrain wire-edge ribbon, 1½" wide

14" very pale pink grosgrain wire-edge ribbon, 1½" wide

24" pale silver metallic ribbon, ¾" wide

20" purple bias-cut silk ribbon, ⁷/₁₆" wide

8" blue ombre picot-edge ribbon, ¼" wide

18" olive green ombre wire-edge ribbon, 1½" wide

12" frosted green wire-edge ribbon, 1" wide

7" celery green ruffled-edge ribbon, ⅝" wide

1" circle of crinoline

4½" circle of crinoline

8 double-headed pink/green stamen buds

12 double-headed tiny yellow stamens

4 pearl seed beads

Steps:

1. Make one large pink cabochon rose. The rose is made in three parts. It has a coil center, surrounded by three inner rolled edge petals and then four outer rolled-edge petals. The coil rose center uses 7" of ⅝" wide dusty pink wired ombre ribbon and the upright coil u-gather technique, diagrams 49 through 51, pages 107 and 108. Stitch this very ruffled coiled center to the middle of a 1" circle of crinoline. All the petals use the rolled edge u-gather technique, diagrams 60 through 63, pages 112 and 113. The first row of three petals use 2½" of 1½" wide pale pink grosgrain wired ribbon per petal. Gather to a length of about 1". The outer four petals use 3½" of 1½" wide very pale pink grosgrain wired ribbon. Gather to a length of about 1½". The petal should cup. Sew the first petal around the coil center. Overlap and sew on the second petal. Overlap and sew on the third petal—all the petals will overlap to fully enclose the rose center. Evenly arrange and sew the outer four petals around the three inner petals.

2. Make four silver folded roses. Each rose uses 6" of ¾" wide pale silver metallic ribbon and the folded rose technique, diagrams 87 through 92, pages 132 and 133.

3. Make four purple blossoms. Each blossom uses 5" of ⁷⁄₁₆" wide purple bias-cut silk ribbon per blossom and the four-petal u-gather technique, diagrams 70 and 71, page 119. Each center has three double-headed yellow stamens folded in half with the stems wrapped together.

4. Make four blue rosettes. Each rosette uses 2" of ¼" wide blue ombre picot-edge ribbon and the u-gather technique, diagrams 40 through 42, page 103. Use one pearl seed bead at the center of each rosette.

5. Make eight mitered leaves. Use the mitered leaf technique, diagrams 137 through 140, page 163. Make four large leaves using 4½" of 1½" wide olive green ombre wire-edge ribbon. Make four small leaves using 3" of 1" wide frosted green wire-edge ribbon.

6. Make four green half-round leaves. Use 1¾" of ⅝" wide ruffled-edge celery green ribbon and the half-round technique, diagram 122, page 154.

7. Make four bunches of stamen buds using two pink /green double-headed stamens per bunch. Fold the stems and wrap them with thread to form a cluster.

Putting the Composition Together:

Refer to the photo for placement of the flowers and leaves. If necessary, turn the page to orient the image to the instructions. Remember to hide all the raw edges by overlapping the leaves and flowers.

1. Using the 4½" circle of crinoline, mark in pencil, the four positions of a clock face: 12, 3, 6, and 9 o'clock. Sew the large mitered leaves at these positions being sure that the tips of the leaves do not extend beyond the crinoline edge.

2. Add the smaller mitered leaves in between the large leaves, so the tips of each almost reach the crinoline edge. The raw edges will be hidden by the large pink rose.

3. Stitch the large cabochon rose at the center.

4. Alternate the four silver folded roses and the purple blossoms in a circle around the rose. Stitch the small celery green half-round leaves under both the purple blossoms and the small mitered leaves.

5. Stitch the blue filler flowers on top of the purple blossoms and celery green leaves.

6. Stitch the stamen bud clusters near the silver folded roses.

7. Cut away the excess crinoline and sew the composition to a project of your choice.

Half dolls were a very popular element in ribbonwork during the 1920s, and they were always used on practical projects such as tea cozies, feather dusters, brushes, lampshades, and, of course, as pincushions. This reproduction half doll with a silk dress is made as a sewing caddy.

You will need:

"Melinda" half doll, 3¾"

6½" wire stand or large pincushion base

½ yd. cream dupioni silk fabric, 54" wide

½ yd. batting, ¼" loft

7" piece embroidered net lace, 9" wide

47" pale green double-faced satin-silk ribbon, ⅜" wide

11" green flower bud trim

43" lavender/green loop trim

48" beige/green silk embroidery ribbon, ½" wide

87" beige/green silk embroidery ribbon, ⅛" wide

26" green/cream picot-edge ribbon, ¼" wide

6" green/yellow ruffled-edge ribbon, ¼" wide

6" blue/cream picot-edge ribbon, ¼" wide

3" purple embroidery silk ribbon, ¼" wide

63" pink/sage embroidery silk ribbon, ¼" wide

29" pink/tan embroidery silk ribbon, ½" wide

12" pink embroidery silk ribbon, ½" wide

9" pink/yellow embroidery silk ribbon, ½" wide

4½" pale gold double-faced satin-silk ribbon, ⅜" wide

3½" tan ruffled-edge ribbon, ¼" wide

4½" pink ruffled-edge ribbon, ½" wide

4½" yellow ruffled-edge ribbon, ½" wide

9" cream pleated georgette ribbon, ⅝" wide

4½" taupe pleated georgette ribbon, ⅝" wide

8" peach/green picot-edge ribbon, ¼" wide

2 snaps

5 gold seed beads

"Melinda" Half Doll Sewing Caddy

If you only want to make the flowers that appear on the apron in this project, then go to the "Make the Flowers and Leaves for the Apron" section. They would most certainly be very nice on other projects.

For those of you wanting to dress a half doll, this very beautiful sewing caddy project will give you all the instructions and directions you need. Choose to make either the four-panel dress, or the simpler tube dress for your doll.

Whether you use a treasured antique half doll or a reproduction doll, adapt the dress size to fit your doll. Delete some of the flowers if you are making the project for a doll smaller than the one described here. The instructions are for a large half doll with a finished project height of 10¼".

Steps for Making the Flowers and Leaves for the Apron:

Before you begin — read the instructions carefully and arrange your ribbons in the order that they will be used. Some ribbons will be used in several places.

1. Make fifteen curved leaves using the curved leaf technique, diagrams 123 through 126, pages 155 and 156. Make three leaves using 2¼" of ⅜" green satin-silk per leaf. Make nine leaves using 1¾" of ¼" wide olive green ombre picot-edge ribbon. Make three leaves using 1¾" of ¼" wide yellow/green ruffled-edge ribbon.

2. Make three blue rosettes using 2¼" of ¼" wide blue ombre picot-edge ribbon and the u-gather technique, diagrams 40 through 42, page 103. Sew a gold seed bead in each center.

3. Make four large ribbon candy roses using 6" each of ½" wide silk embroidery ribbon. Review the Ribbon Candy Rose Exercise in Chapter 5, page 77. Make two roses using the ½" wide pink/tan silk ribbon. Use one rose on the right side of the apron and one at the top of the apron. Make two roses using the pink silk ribbon. Use one rose on the left side of the apron and one in the center of the taupe rose.

4. Make four folded roses. Refer to the folded rose technique, diagrams 87 through 92, pages 132 and 133. Make two roses using 4½" of ½" wide pink/yellow silk ribbon and use as centers for the cream rose and the yellow rose. Make one rose using 4½" of ½" wide pink/tan silk ribbon and use in the center of the pink rose. Make one rose using 4½" of ⅜" wide gold satin-silk and use in the center of the gold rose.

5. Make two folded roses with gathered extensions using 4" each of ¼" wide peach picot-edge ribbon and diagram 93, page 134. Trim the raw ends of one rose closely and stitch it to the center of the cream upright rose. Use the other on it's own on the apron.

6. Make the outer petals for the six combination roses. There are three roses with rosette ruffles, two roses with double rosette ruffles, and one upright coiled rose. Use the u-gather technique and variations.

⁂ Make one rosette ruffle (diagrams 40 through 42, page 103) using 3½" of ¼" wide tan ruffled-edge ribbon and insert the gold satin folded rose into the center.

⁂ Make one rosette (diagrams 40 through 42, page 103) using 4½" of ½" wide pink ruffled-edge ribbon and insert the pink/tan folded rose into the center.

⁂ Make one rosette (diagrams 40 through 42, page 103) using 4½" of ½" wide yellow ruffled-edge ribbon and insert the pink/yellow folded rose into the center.

⁂ Make one double rosette ruffle (bottom ⅔ fold, diagrams 52 through 54, page 109) using 4½" of the ⅝" wide cream pleated ribbon and insert the other pink/yellow folded rose into the center.

⁂ Make one double rosette ruffle (bottom ⅔ fold, diagrams 52 through 54, page 109) using 4½" of the ⅝" wide taupe pleated ribbon. Use under the pink/tan ribbon candy rose.

⁂ Make one upright coil u-gather (diagrams 49 through 51, page 107 and 108) using 4½" of ⅝" wide cream pleated ribbon and insert the picot-edged peach rose into the center.

Steps for Decorating the Dress and Pockets:

1. If not using a wire stand, make a tube pincushion base, referring to Chapter 10 Pincushion Method 2, page 172.

2. Make a four-panel self-lined, padded skirt, a self-lined apron; and two self-lined pockets as described in Chapter 10, Skirt Method 2, page 176. Increase the patterns 200%.

3. Decorate the bottom of the skirt hem. Ruche 48" of ½" wide beige/green embroidery ribbon. Refer to straight ruching diagram 18, page 76. To assist in ruching this quantity of ribbon, divide the ribbon into four quarters and pin each quarter mark to a seam on the skirt. Ruche the ribbon in one segment and then come back and sew the ribbon in that segment to the dress. Repeat for each segment. Hand sew 22" to 23" of lavender/green loop trim on top of, and at the center of, the ruched silk ribbon.

4. If you made pockets for your skirt, the closed size is about 2½" tall by 3" wide. Trim the pocket flaps with 5½" each of lavender/green loop trim. For the flap of each pocket, make a shoelace bow using 9" of ⅛" wide beige/green silk ribbon. Pin the bow into a pleasing shape and then stitch into place. Make two rosettes (u-gather diagrams 40 through

42, page 103) using 3" of ¼" wide pink/sage silk ribbon, and 3" of ¼" wide purple silk ribbon. Sew a gold seed bead to the center of each, and sew to the green ribbon tape on the open pocket.

5. Make four curved leaves using 1¾" of ¼" wide olive green ombre picot-edge ribbon and the curved leaf diagrams 123 through 126, pages 155 and 156. Sew two leaves to each pocket flap. Make two pink ribbon candy roses using 6" of ½" wide pink silk ribbon for each rose. Refer to the Ribbon Candy Rose Exercise in Chapter 5, page 77. Sew the roses over the leaves. Sew a snap to each pocket flap. Sew the closed pocket on the right of the skirt, just above the hem trimmings, and centered in between the skirt seams. On the "open" pocket sew in the 2¼" x 1¾" piece of felt for the needle pad and trim it with 8½" of lavender/green loop trim. Sew a ribbon tape across the middle of the open pocket using about 4" of ⅜" green silk-satin ribbon. Sew two silk rosettes (see step 4) to the ribbon tape. This tape will hold a needle threader. Sew the "open" pocket to the left of the skirt.

6. Make twenty mini ribbon candy roses using 3" of ¼" wide pink/sage silk ribbon. Review the Ribbon Candy Rose Exercise in Chapter 5, page 77. Make twenty figure 8 loop leaves using the Figure 8 technique, diagrams 29 and 30, page 83, and 2¼" of ⅛" wide beige/green silk ribbon for each. Place one mini ribbon candy rose on one figure 8 leaf. Evenly arrange and sew in place the twenty mini ribbon candy roses/figure eight leaf combos onto the skirt. You might have two roses left over. Put one in the bow on the doll's hat if desired or stitch them to the back of the dress or the top of the apron.

7. Before you put the dress on the doll, hand-sew the outer fabric to the lining in the 2" seam opening. Run a gathering stitch around the dress waist, but do not tighten yet. Put the dress over the doll's head. Position the dress so the seam opening is at the back and to one side of the doll. The pockets will be on the sides of the doll. Check for dress length. Trim excess fabric from the top of the dress as needed. Tighten the gathering at the waist and secure. Sew the back seam opening closed. Cover the waist with 4" to 6" of the ⅜" wide green satin-silk ribbon. Stitch (or lightly glue) in place.

Steps for Decorating and Finishing the Apron:

1. Make a bow using 24" of ⅛" wide beige/green ribbon. Pin the bow into shape, and then stitch it in place to the apron front.

2. Tack 11" of the "leaf" green flower bud trim to the top of the bow, so the tails trail down to the apron edges. Arrange the ribbon flowers as shown in the photo and sew to the lace/fabric.

3. Turn up the bottom of the apron hem and hand-finish. Put the apron against the doll's waist to decide the length of the apron. Trim off excess fabric from the top of the apron as needed, leaving a ½" to turn in. Turn in the top edges and hand sew closed. Gather the top of the apron so it neatly fits between the center panel seams on the front of the dress.

4. Sew 30" of ⅜" wide silk-satin green ribbon to the waistband of the apron. Tie the apron onto the doll and finish in a shoelace bow at the back.

Bibliography

Ben-Yusuf, Anna. *Edwardian Hats*. R.L. Shep, 1992, originally published 1909.

Druesedow, Jean L. *In Style*. Metropolitan Museum of Art.

Hopkins, Susie. *The Century of Hats*. Chartwell Books, 1999.

Kaye, Georgina Kerr. *Millinery For Every Woman*. Berkeley, CA: Lacis Publications, 1992; originally published 1926.

Lorrin, Shona and Marc. *The Half Doll, Vols 1, 2, and 3*. Walsworth Publishing Company, 1999, 2001, and 2004.

Marion, Frieda and Norma Werner. *The Collector's Encyclopedia of Half Dolls*. Crown Publishers, Inc., 1979.

Martin, Gene Allen. *Make Your Own Hats*. Boston: Houghton Mifflin Company, 1921.

Old Fashioned Ribbon Art. New York: Dover Publications, Inc., 1986.

Picken, Mary Brooks. *Old Fashioned Ribbon Trimmings and Flowers*. New York: Dover Publications, 1993; originally published 1922.

Ribbon and Fabric Trimmings. Woman's Institute of Domestic Arts and Sciences, Inc., 1925.

Ribbon Art, Vol 1 No. 1. Ribbon Art Publishing Co, Inc., 1923.

Ribbon Art, Vol 1 No. 2. Ribbon Art Publishing Company of America, Inc.

Ribbon Art, Vol 1 No. 3. Ribbon Art Publishing Company of America, Inc.

LEFT: Ribbon bookmarks are an easy and fun way to share your love of ribbon with a friend. Simply select some pretty ribbons that co-ordinate and join them together with either fusible webbing or tacky glue, or, of course, stitch them. Add some little fuchsias, rosettes, roses, or a tassel.

Resources

Retail

Helen Gibb Design, Inc.
1002 Turnberry Circle
Louisville, CO 80027
Web Site: www.helengibb.com
E-mail: helen@helengibb.com
Phone: 303-673-0949
Fax: 303-926-0065

All the ribbonwork supplies and ribbons used in this book are available through Helen Gibb Design. The full line includes: needles, thread, crinoline, ribbons, ribbon starter kits, trims, pre-made flowers, porcelain half dolls and kits, box kits, memory albums and journals, silk prints, laces, and much more. Signed copies of Helen's books are also available; to purchase them, visit www.helengibb.com.

Helen teaches ribbon workshops internationally, and within the USA. She also has an annual ribbon retreat in the fabulous Colorado Rocky Mountains. Please visit her web site www.helengibb.com, for more information and to buy ribbonwork supplies online.

Send $6 if requesting a product brochure, and $6 for a ribbon brochure, and two first class stamps, to Helen Gibb Design, Inc. at the address above.

Wholesale

Artemis, Inc.
Phone: 1-888-233-5187
The largest and best source for the famous
Hanah Silk bias-cut silk ribbons. Call for
information.

Renaissance Ribbons
PO Box 699
Oregon House, CA 95962
Internet: www.renaissanceribbons.com
Phone: 530-692-0842
Fax: 530-692-0915
Importer of high quality French ribbons.

Mokuba
55 West 39th Street
New York, NY 10018
Phone: 212-869-8900
Fax: 212-869-8970
Importer of beautiful Japanese ribbons and
flower trims.

Quilters' Resource, Inc.
2211 N. Elston
Chicago, Il 60614
Phone 1-773-278-5695
French ribbons and trims,
crinoline, milliners needles,
flowerhead pins, and fine twisted
beading thread.

Other

Krause Publications
700 East State St.
Iola, WI 54990-0001
Phone: 888-457-2873
Internet: www.krause.com

Sara Frances, photographer
Important Occasions Photography
1801 S. Pearl St
Denver, CO 80210
Phone: 303-744-1807
Internet: www.sarafrancesphotography.com

Karen Wallach, illustrator
657 Clarkson
Denver, CO 80218

Index

Bachelor button 80
Basic bud 124-125
Beads 34
Bellflower 94, 97
Berries 94-96
Blossom 79
Boat leaf 157-159
Boué Soeurs 15
Bows 82-85
    Creating 67, 82-85
    Figure 8 loop 83
    Finger 84
    Milliners 85
    Shoelace 83
Calyxes 60-61
Cardboard, covering 37, 177, 178
Carnation 28, 80
Chrysanthemum 73
Cornflower 80
Crinoline 15, 35
Curved leaf 155-156
Cut flowers 90
Daisy 72
Decorative Stitches and Trimmings 24
Delphinium 91
Dipped corner petal 136-137
Dyeing ribbon 169-170
    Brushed wet-into-wet 170
    Dip dyeing 170
    Edge dyed 170
    Graduated dyeing 170
    Pre-made ribbon flowers 170

Floral tape 37
Fuchsia 126-127
Glue 38
Gothic arch leaf 164-165
Gothic arch petal 147
Half doll 26, 27, 171-176
    Pincushion 172
    Project 240-247
    Round base 172
    Skirt pattern 174, 175-176
    Tube-shaped base 173
Half-boat leaf 160-161
Half-round leaf 154
Hydrangea 92
Jardinière 195-197, 216-219
Leaves 151-165
    Boat 157-159
    Curved 155-156
    Gothic arch 164-165
    Half-boat 160-161
    Half-round 154
    Mitered 162-163
    Prairie point 152-153
Lily 184-185
Loops 67, 82
    Creating 67, 82
    Multiple 82
    Single 82
Metallic laces and trims 21, 29
Mitered leaf 162-163
Needle, milliners 34
Pansy 117, 179

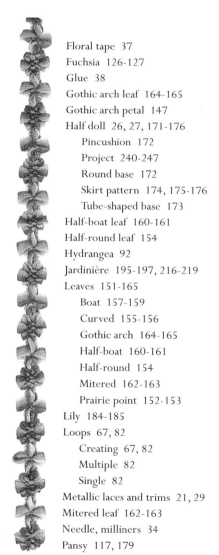

Peony 80
Petals 103-105, 136-147
    Dipped corner 136-137
    Gothic arch 147
    Pinch 144-146
    Rolled corner 138-140
Pinch petal 144-146
Pincushion 17, 38, 198-200
Pins 35
Prairie point leaf 152-153
Projects – easy 180-205
    Cell phone case 192-194
    Leigh powder patter 181-183
    Lily 184-185
    Lipstick pouch 192, 194
    Mixed large roses in a jardinière
        195-197
    Pinecone ornament 190-191
    Purple hat with coil rose 188-189
    Rosebud boutonniere 204-205
    Rosette boutonniere 204-205
    Sachets with blossom flowers 186-187
    Tin can pincushion 198-200
    Wedding bouquet 201-203
Projects – more challenging 206-247
    Bias-cut silk flowers 227-229
    Circle/square design project 238-239
    C-shape design project 234-237
    Jardinière with roses 216-219
    Melinda half doll 240-247
    Ribbon board 224-226
    Rose pendant 210, 212
    Small flowers on lace 220-223
    Spring brooch 213-215

    Vintage brooch 207-209
    Vintage style ribbon flowers 230-233
    Wild hairy pendant 210-211
Ribbon 41
    Bias-cut silk 44
    Combining techniques 179
    Creating loops and bows 67, 82-85
    Double faced 44
    Dyeing 169-170
    Folding 123, 124
    Gathering 67, 80-81
    Jacquard 44, 45
    Knotting 67, 70-71
    Non-wired 44
    Pleating 67, 86-87
    Ruching 67, 75-79
    Shirring 67, 74
    Silk-satin 44
    Twisting 67, 68-69
    Vintage 19
    Wire-edge 42
Ribbon and Fabric Trimmings 24
Ribbon Art 23, 25
Ribbon Art Publishing Company 24, 27
Ribbon guides
    Basic bud 124
    Bell flowers 97
    Berries and rosehips 95
    Blossoms and continuous petals 118
    Boat leaf 157
    Cabochon rose 114
    Curved leaf 156
    Dipped corner petals 137
    Edge gathering 80

Flat rose 105
Fuchsia 126
Gothic arch leaf 164
Half-boat leaf 160
Half-round leaf 154
Knotting 71
Knotting loops 71
Pinch petals 144
Prairie point leaf 152
Ribbon candy rose 77
Rolled corner petals 140
Tube calyx 60
Upright rose or rosette 107
Vintage flat rose 128
Ribbonwork, definition 15
Rolled corner petal 138-140
Roses
    Cabochon 30, 112-113, 114, 179
    Coil 31, 106-108, 189
    Flat rosette 103-105
    Fantasy 179
    Folded 131-133, 134, 135
    Ribbon 29
    Ribbon candy 77
    Tea 142-143, 179
    Upright rosette 106-108
    Vintage flat 128-130
    Wild 179
Rosehips 94-96
Sachets 186-187
Scissors 36
Silk ribbon embroidery, definition 17
Stamens 39, 56-59
    Stemmed 58-59

Unstemmed 56-57
Stem cover 94, 98
Stems 62-65
    Bias-cut silk ribbon covered 63
    Covering 62
    Floral tape covered 62
    Thread-covered 63
    Tube stem cover 64-65
Stitches 51-53
    Backstitch 51
    Gathering stitch 52
    Running stitch 52
    Stab stitch 52
    Stitch length 53
Tailor's awl 36
Thread, beading 34
Tips, beginning 50
Tubes 94
Tulip 148-149
U-gather 101-121
    Bottom ⅔ fold 109, 121
    Continuous 115-121
    Five-petal 120
    Four-petal 118-119
    Rolled edge 112-113
    Single 103-114
    Three-petal 116
    Top fold 110-111, 121
    Two-petal 115
Violet 117, 179
Wire, thread-covered 37
Woman's Institute of Domestic Arts
    and Sciences 24

About the Author

Helen was born in Sydney, Australia, and now lives in the United States of America.

"Growing up in Australia during the 1950s and 1960s, I wasn't particularly interested in sewing or embroidery," says Helen. "The only sewing project I finished in primary school was a shower cap and an apron!"

Helen's ribbonwork journey started in the late 1990s with the purchase of an Edwardian driving hat, and later, a black mourning bonnet complete with black ribbon embellishments. An antique book on old millinery techniques was also purchased and in the back of that book were some simplified instructions on how to make a ribbon rose. Since then, Helen has acquired several old books about ribbonwork and some lovely samples of vintage ribbon flowers and items from the 1920s, many of which are shown on the pages of this book.

With a vast store of self taught ribbon techniques and access to ribbons from France, Japan, and Germany, Helen's talents in ribbonwork are evident throughout the pages of this book and her other two ribbon books—*The Secrets of Fashioning Ribbon Flowers*, and *Heirloom Ribbonwork*.

Helen's ribbonwork has been showcased in numerous magazines, including *Better Homes and Gardens*, and *Doll Costuming* in the USA, and *Embroidery and Cross Stitch Magazine* in Australia. In addition, Helen is a regular guest on HGTV's *The Carol Duvall Show*, and she appears on PBS's *Creative Living*, and on network TV news programs in Denver.

Helen lives in Colorado with her husband Jim, where they enjoy the Rocky Mountains. When not doing ribbonwork, Helen loves to read and solve crossword puzzles. She also sings with the Rocky Mountain Chorale.

Visit Helen's web site, www.helengibb.com, for ribbonwork supplies and more information about ribbonwork.

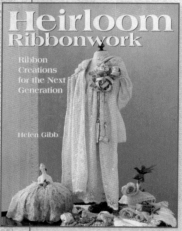
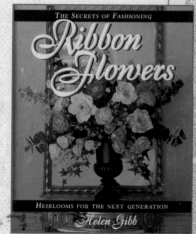